50 Maestros, 50 Recordings

THE BEST OF INDIAN CLASSICAL MUSIC

Amaan Ali Khan   Ayaan Ali Khan

An Imprint of HarperCollins *Publishers*

First published in India in 2009 by Collins
An imprint of HarperCollins *Publishers* India
a joint venture with
The India Today Group

ISBN: 978-81-7223-918-3

2 4 6 8 10 9 7 5 3 1

HarperCollins Publishers
A-53, Sector 57, NOIDA, Uttar Pradesh – 201301, India
77-85 Fulham Palace Road, London W6 8JB, United Kingdom
Hazelton Lanes, 55 Avenue Road, Suite 2900, Toronto, Ontario M5R 3L2
and 1995 Markham Road, Scarborough, Ontario M1B 5M8, Canada
25 Ryde Road, Pymble, Sydney, NSW 2073, Australia
31 View Road, Glenfield, Auckland 10, New Zealand
10 East 53rd Street, New York NY 10022, USA

Typeset in 10.5/14 Bembo
Jojy Philip New Delhi - 15

Printed and bound at
Thomson Press (India) Ltd.

To our grandfather
Ustad Haafiz Ali Khan,
for whom
music was life
and
life was music

Authors' Note

It has been an ecstatic experience to hear fifty hours of sheer magic all over again. For us, this book has been a journey back in time as this is what we have grown up on and grown up with. The list of artistes in this book is in no way an evaluation or rating of their work or of them as artistes but it is a list that has without doubt influenced Indian classical music as it stands today.

We have tried our very best to address each artiste in all humility, however, we have not repeatedly used decorations like Ustad, Pandit, Sahib and ji too often. This is simply for the reader's convenience and in no way marks any disrespect to these artistes from our end.

This book is our salutation to these fifty icons of music. Thank you for what you have done for music and for music lovers.

AMAAN ALI KHAN
AYAAN ALI KHAN

Contents

Introduction xv
Know Your Classical Music xxi

Ustad Abdul Halim Jaffer Khan 1
Ustad Abdul Karim Khan 4
Ustad Ahmed Jaan Thirakhwa 7
Ustad Ali Akbar Khan 11
Ustad Amir Khan 15
Ustad Amjad Ali Khan 18
Dr Balamurali Krishna 24
Ustad Bade Ghulam Ali Khan 28
Begum Akhtar 32
Pandit Bhimsen Joshi 35
Ustad Bismillah Khan 38
D.K. Pattammal 44
Pandit D.V. Paluskar 50
Ustad Enayat Khan 54
Ustad Faiyaz Khan 57
Dr Gangubai Hangal 60
Ustad Ghulam Mustafa Khan 63
Girija Devi 67
Ustad Haafiz Ali Khan 71

Pandit Hari Prasad Chaurasia 76
Ustad Imdad Khan 79
Pandit Jasraj 83
Surashri Kesarbai Kerkar 86
Pandit Kishan Maharaj 89
Kishori Amonkar 92
Pandit Kumar Gandharva 96
Dr L. Subramaniam 99
Maharajapuram V. Santhanam 102
M.L. Vasanthakumari 106
Mogubai Kurdikar 110
M.S. Subbulakshmi 114
Pandit Nikhil Banerjee 118
Pandit Omkarnath Thakur 121
Begum Parveen Sultana 125
Ustad Rais Khan 129
Pandit Ravi Shankar 133
S. Balachander 137
Pandit Samta Prasad 144
Semmangudi R. Srinivasa Iyer 147
Pandit Shiv Kumar Sharma 151
Shobha Gurtu 154
T.R. Mahalingam 157
Pandit V.G. Jog 159
Ustad Vilayat Khan 163

DUETS 167

Ustad Alla Rakha and Ustad Zakir Hussain 169
Pandit Bhimsen Joshi and Dr Balamurali Krishna 173
Ustad Bismillah Khan and Ustad Amjad Ali Khan 176

Ustad Ali Akbar Khan and Pandit Ravi Shankar 180
Ustad Rais Khan and Ustad Sultan Khan......................... 183
Ustad Vilayat Khan and Ustad Bismillah Khan 186

Afterword.. 189
Acknowledgements 193

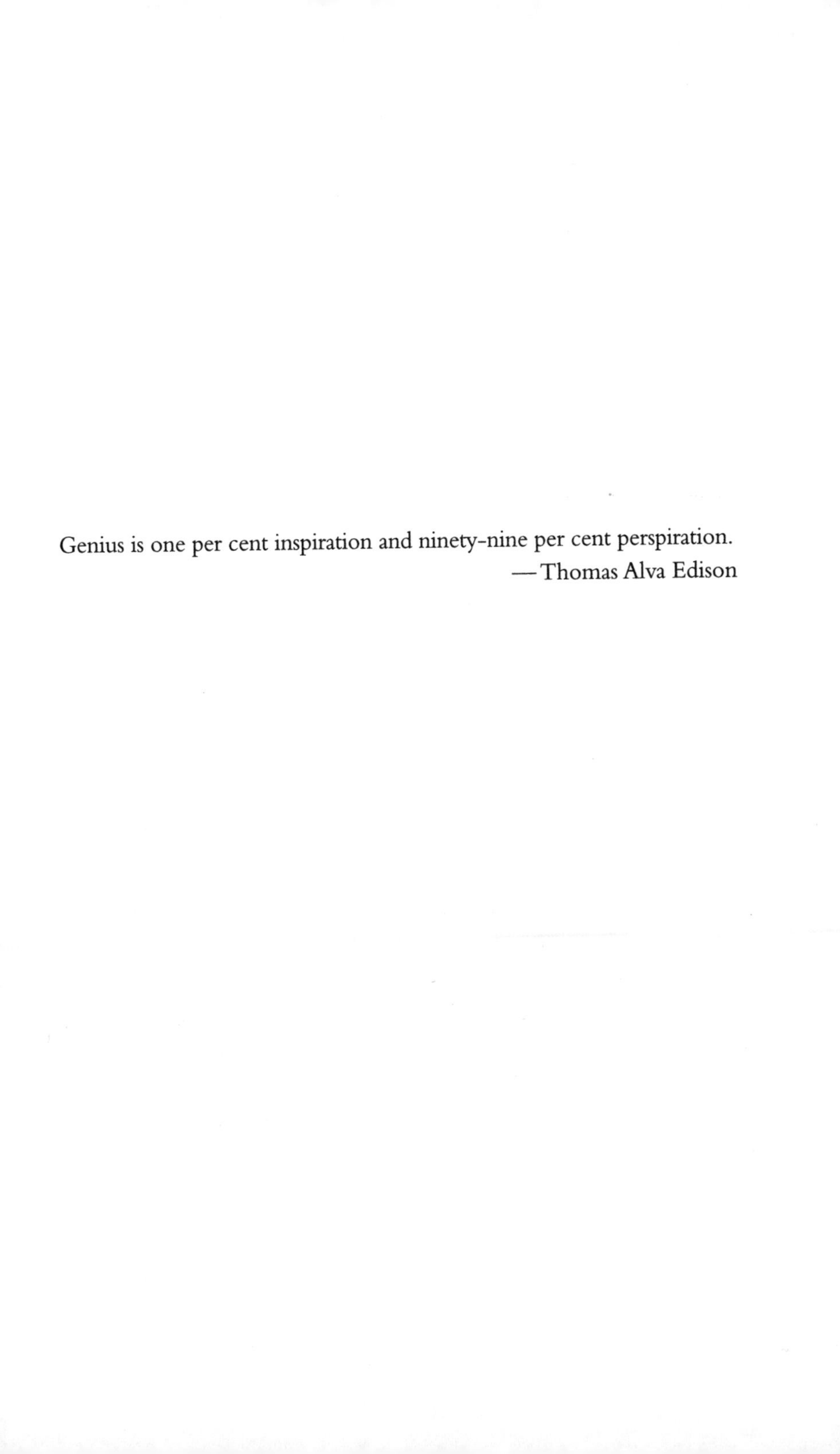

Genius is one per cent inspiration and ninety-nine per cent perspiration.

—Thomas Alva Edison

Introduction

When we were born, two years apart from each other, our father sang in our ears from the moment we were placed in his lap. Perhaps our musical training began that day itself. When you are born into a home where the language spoken is music, where every brick of the house is soaked in music, it is only natural to get involved, drenched and completely absorbed into the fascinating world of twelve notes.

When we were growing up, our father would always be very happy to see us listen to music, not just practise it. Not just his own music, but the music of an entire range of artistes from the era of our grandfather to the contemporaries of our father. We were never asked to listen to a particular artiste, or not to listen to another; to listen only to classical music and not listen to the music of the West or Bollywood. The choice and the freedom was entirely ours. But it is only natural to be influenced by the music that your guru speaks of or refers to when he plays. We thus became engrossed in the world of Indian classical music that our father had grown up with, along with our own contemporary choices.

It isn't easy to shortlist the works of only fifty artistes in the oceanic journey of Indian classical music. However, there were a few who were the pillars of their time and who have today become responsible for shaping the very existence of Indian classical music. There are numerous musicians who have made a difference but for us, these are the names that stand out. These were names then and are names now that no music label or music festival can do without. These are also the artistes we have

Our father teaching the two of us, beneath our grandfather's portrait

grown up listening to and who have shaped us to be the musicians that we are today. We were very lucky to have had immediate access to most of our father's contemporaries right from childhood. We have spent memorable moments with many of them and, in the course of time, many relationships have also changed for the better or for the worse.

The bitter truth is that after these musicians, the golden era of geniuses is over. Every artiste we have heard after this list of artistes is a byproduct of these great masters. The recordings only prove this observation. These selected artistes and recordings are in fact the sources from which the present younger generation of artistes has extracted its favourite things. Today, we clearly lack originality and ideas. Artistes who are barely in their early twenties are in a rush to be called maestros, and artistes who have just started performing with their progenies want to be called living legends. The comical irony is that the real geniuses in the world of classical music make it a point not to use decorations in their names! There is a lack of respect between artistes today and a callous attitude towards senior artistes, which makes us very sad. There is even a lack of consistency in relationships, to the extent of artistes addressing each other differently each time they meet. Egos and insecurities have taken over passion and integrity. But we continue to hope that our generation is able not just to take forward the message of Indian classical music but also to continue its very essence and existence as a way of life.

To be a musician is itself a blessing as you are not really answerable to anyone but yourself. For those few hours when you are on stage, you are in a creative frenzy, sometimes supernaturally unreal. There are times when you get off stage only to realize that something special happened up there on stage that day. It is a blessing to be in a profession where you love doing what you do. It is also a non-debatable factor that music is indeed the best way to connect to that supreme power that we have never seen. Be it any religion, music has always been the pathway to spirituality.

The term 'young artiste' often amused us as we had started performing from the age of eight and more professionally from about eleven and thirteen, and artistes who were touching fifty were also called 'young artistes' or 'the next generation'. We saw many things when we started touring overseas from 1989 in Europe (Logan Hall, London) and 1991 in the US (Asia Society) and our first tour had a mixed impact on the two of us at our age. We felt very fortunate to be playing in great venues because of our father but we also saw a parallel world of unknown artistes and condescending organizers who would refuse to provide hotel rooms and make the artistes stay at people's houses, drive on their own and even clean up after a house concert. These were the rules of the tour and every artiste who has gone overseas has had to do this at some point and struggle to make ends meet. It is far from the more glamorous worlds of other forms of art.

Back home, we once refused to perform when we arrived at our concert venue and discovered that there was no platform on the stage. This was for an institution that propagated classical music among students but we felt that the principles were somewhat lost. When we put our foot down the answer was that 'even Pandit so-and-so sang without any complaints.' Obviously we didn't succumb to that but this was the attitude. We eventually went on stage only after the platform was made.

Often one wonders why a talented artiste many a time doesn't create a buzz and on the other hand, someone with minimal talent sells like hot cakes — well, there is no answer. The answer is written by a greater power. There is no good music or bad music. Everyone gives or at least tries to give his or her best but the magic wand is held by that all time magician, the power, the heavens, the almighty.

An issue that our father has been fighting over for years is about the division of Indian music into Hindustani and Carnatic. Is Carnatic not Hindustani, or rather, a part of Hindustan? We cannot agree with him more. Though we are aware that the systems are different, they are indeed the same twelve notes. Why do we not address them as the classical music of north India and south India? Some great duets have also taken place between artistes from both the systems who have found a common meeting point. However, over time it has become too predictable. There also always seems to be an ugly undercurrent between artistes from both systems even as they collaborate together. However, there are also some grand works between masters from both the systems.

Indian classical music has had a very spiritual and scientific development and growth. This was a phenomenon that existed from the Vedic times. The tradition of classical music dates back to the Sam Veda period. The earliest version of classical music were the Vedic chants. Interestingly, the effects of all twelve notes on our body, mind and soul are completely scientific. If we sing out all the twelve notes with concentration, the human body receives positive vibrations. In fact, the positive effect transcends to plants and animals. Various permutations and combinations give the scales the shape of a raga. But a raga is much more and beyond. It's not just a mere scale. A raga has to be invoked, understood and cared for, like a living entity. People might find it amusing but in the old days and even to some extent now, artistes would say, 'Don't mess with a raga — it can curse you!'

North Indian classical music owes itself to several legends over the period of time. The central figures include Swami Haridas, Mian Tansen, Baiju Bawra, Hazrat Amir Khusru and many others. As north

Indian classical music has always been an oral tradition, not much was written or documented. What has been passed down is through voices and instruments, by listening and thus learning. There are many conventions and traditions, but no single set of rules. Presentation is completely personal. Our grandfather, for instance, never played a raga beyond twenty-five minutes as he felt that it was all repetition after that. Then came a time when the longer the concert was, the greater you were considered. The world of rhythm, too, has been highly developed. Today taals vary from 9½ beats to 13¼ beats to 25 beats.

The fascinating history of south Indian classical music can be traced back to Vedic times. The earliest recorded documents of south Indian classical music are said to have existed in Bharata's *Natyashashtra* (2 BC–2 AD), Matanga's *Brihaddesi* (5th century) and in Saranga Deva's *Sangita Ratnakara* (13th century). But the pillars that contributed to and developed this system of music were Purandara Dasa and the musical trinity of Thyagaraja Swami, Shyama Shastri and Muthuswami Dikshitar. In Carnatic music there are 72 Melakarta ragas. These are the parent scales that have all seven notes both in the ascent and descent. The first 36 ragas have sudha madhyamam and the remaining 36 have prati madhyamam svara. Each sudha madhyamam raga has a corresponding prati madhyamam raga. There are seven major talas known as the sapta soolaadi talas. These are rendered by finger counts, beats and waves of the palm. Each tala has five varieties, i.e. tisra (3), chatusrasra (4), khanda (5), misra (7) and sankeerna (9).

Carnatic music is primarily based on musical compositions which are devotional in nature. These have different musical structures and are divided into musical forms with three main sections known as the Pallavi, Anupallavi and Charanam. The musical forms include Geetam, Svarajati, Varnam, Kriti, Ragam-Tanam-Pallavi, Padam, Javali, Tillana and more. Geetam, Varnam and Svarajati are made up of compositions which are intended for the practice of music and are termed Abhyaasa Gaana, while Kriti, Ragam-Tanam-Pallavi, Padam, Javali, Tillana, etc. are best suited for concerts and figure under Sabha Gaana. Varnam and some Svarajatis are more serious compositions which are also rendered in concerts.

Varnas and kritis are pre-composed and highly evolved compositions which give a complete Raga Svaroopa. These compositions are replete with the essence of the raga and bring out every nuance of the raga and its inherent beauty. Hence, in order to fully understand a raga, it is essential to learn the maximum number of compositions,especially the kritis composed by the trinity. The extempore music or the Manodharma Sangeeta includes Raga Alapana (elaboration of melody without words), Taanam (developing a raga with syllables like nom, tom, anamta, etc.), Niraval (musical elaboration of an appropriate theme) and Kalpana Svaras (svara improvisation). Kritis and ragam-tanam-pallavi are most suited for extempore music and the creative genius of a musician lies in his mastery over this music.

Although Carnatic instrumental music is a unique tradition in itself with the use of instruments like the veena, violin, flute, nadaswaram, gottuvadyam, etc., they revolve around the instrumental interpretations of vocal forms. The concert tradition of playing varnam, kritis with alapana, niraval and kalapana svaras, ragam-tanam-pallavi and tillana are elements common to both vocal and instrumental music in southern India.

In this book, we have tried our best not to be too technical as we feel that good music can only be felt. You do not need to understand it theoretically, just as you don't need to be an art student to appreciate the *Mona Lisa*. One must also know that no artiste who has made it big today is the product of a musical institution. All the stalwarts today have learnt after surrendering, believing and having faith in their guru. Many in life question a guru, many go to many gurus but then the result becomes evident. You are an item that belongs to no one.

It is indeed an honour and a pleasure for us to list a selection of works from the very jewels of our country and we hope that this music that we grew up listening to makes a difference to all your lives as artistes, as music enthusiasts and also as connoisseurs of excellence. However, they were great masters in their own right. Needless to say, these works are what we as artistes felt were their very best. We are sure that each of these artistes has many other priceless jewels in their treasury.

Know Your Classical Music

It can often get very confusing and overwhelming for people to get used to certain terms used in Indian classical music. But it is easy to explain them in simple ways, as music has always been taught in the oral tradition and the art and discipline passed verbally from guru to shishya. The first and most important element of Indian classical music is the raga.

A **Raga** is made of a set of ascending and descending notes within a certain discipline. But it is much more than a scale which also refers to the set of notes. A raga has distinctive features with prominent notes, combinations of notes and timings of the day and season. The north Indian system has ragas for every time of day. Although there is no logical explanation as to why a particular raga must be performed at a particular time, it is traditionally believed that the cycle of sound in every raga affects human behaviour. Each hour of the day represents a different stage of development in human life and is associated with a certain kind of emotion. The correlation is important, as the aim of a raga is to evoke human sentiment. However, this theory does not exist in the south Indian system where there is no specific timing for any raga. In fact, when performing in the south, many north Indian artistes also take the liberty of presenting ragas from any time of the day at any given time. Another interesting difference between north and south is that many ragas are known by different names in either tradition. For instance, Malkauns is called Hindolam in the south, Bhopali is

Mohanam and Yaman is Kalyani. Of course, there are many common names too, like Sindhu Bhairavi, Abhogi, Vachaspati and Kirwani.

Music all over the world is based on seven basic, primary notes which are called the **Shuddha** (literally, pure) notes in Indian classical music, and five **Komal** notes, which are flat. The seven notes are Saraj, Rishabh, Gandhar, Madhyam, Pancham, Dhaiwat and Nishad, or, more simply, Sa Re Ga Ma Pa Dha Ni. In this book we have indicated the flat notes in small letters. Altogether there are twelve notes. A raga may have either the shuddha or komal version of a particular note, or it may use both komal and shuddha. For example, Malkauns and Bilaskhani Todi use only komal notes whereas ragas like Tilak Kamod and Durga have shuddha notes and ragas like Ahir Bhairav and Kirwani use both komal and Shuddh. Some ragas have all seven notes, be it shuddha or komal, while others have five and some even three. The most prominent note in a raga is called **Vaadi** and the second most important note of the raga is called **Samvaadi**.

The traditional style of music which today has become somewhat rare is called **Dhrupad**, where the use of embellishments does not exist. The usage was more of long glides both for vocalists and instrumentalists. On the other hand, **Khayal** is the more prominent and popular style of classical vocal today and has developed greatly over time. Khayal literally means imagination, a thought. The khayal style has largely dominated the vocal music scene for the past several decades. This style gave performers the opportunity and the challenge to display the depth and breadth of their musical knowledge and skill. Khayal is the genre of improvisational music, and hence it is the study of an artistes' imaginative individuality and ability to render a unique khayal at each presentation. Dhrupad, on the other hand, was very rigid. Both these styles of vocal music have had instrumental interpretation over time.

A raga is set to a particular rhythm cycle, called **Taal.** There are different types of taal, the most common being the Teentaal, set to 16 beats (4 + 4 + 4 + 4). Ustad Ahmed Jaan Thirakhwa (see Chapter 3) describes the different forms and styles of rhythm with interesting detail and demonstration.

A raga traditionally opens with a slow elaboration of its notes and movements. This unaccompanied prelude is called the **Alaap** and it serves as an introduction to the raga. It is made up of very slow movements and can be a heavy dose for the newcomer to classical music. In instrumental music, the alaap may end with a **Jor**, whereby a rhythm is created without an accompaniment, through the drone strings. The alaap is usually followed by the **Gat** which is a composition in instrumental and vocal music, though in the rhythmic world it also refers to a style common in the purab style of tabla playing. The gat may be played or sung in a very slow tempo or **Vilambit**, or it may have a very fast composition, which is called **Drut**. The use of different rhythmic patterns is called **Layakari.**

A crescendo or **Jhala** is commonly used to conclude the raga. It is a fast rhythmic style of instrumental music characterized by a constant plucking of the drone strings or **Chikari.** In vocal music, of course, there is no crescendo but usually the musician ends with a taan.

The common structure in Carnatic music is the **Ragam**, **Tanam** and **Pallavi** which are common to both vocal and instrumental music. The performance is mainly divided into three sections which are the pallavi (a single line composition), anupallavi (second section of any composition) and charanam (usually the last section of a composition which is sung or played after the anupallavi). Although Carnatic instrumental music is a unique tradition in itself with the use of instruments like the veena, violin, nadarswaram, etc., the musical tradition revolves around instrumental interpretations of vocal forms. The nuances of the raga are unfolded with the **Varnam** or description, and **Kritis**, which are fixed musical compositions by great composers, are also played or sung. **Niruval** and **Kalpana Swara** provide the opportunity to improvise.

Within its basic structure a raga has many embellishments. **Gamak** is a variation in the pitch of a note, using vigorous oscillations between bordering and distant notes. A fast run of musical notes is called a **Taan**. There are many schools of taan in both vocal and instrumental music. Every school has its own unique technique and pattern. Similar to taans are the **Boltaans** in vocal music, which are embellishments based on the lyrics. Another feature special to vocal music is the **Thumri**, a semi-classical style of singing that deals mainly with lyricism and romantic text. Thumris have lyrics like 'Kya karoo sajni', 'Aye na baalam',

'Kaun gali gayo shyam', etc. A style of poetic recitation that speaks of human emotion, mainly romance or pain, in its lyrics is called **Ghazal**. Another semi-classical style of singing is **Dadra**, which was traditionally accompanied by the **Dadra Taal,** a common six-beat taal used in light and semi-classical vocal and instrumental music.

A raga may be performed from start to finish along these lines, but there is enough space for variety. A **Sawal Jawab** is a question-and-answer session between two instrumentalists, two vocalists or between an instrumentalist/vocalist and a percussionist. A duet between two instrumentalists or vocalists, or a vocalist and an instrumentalist is called a **Jugalbandi**. One must bear in mind that a duet should be a duet and not a duel! When an artiste presents numerous ragas one after the other, like a 'mala' or garland, it is called a **Ragamala** or **Ragamallika**. This term is also closely associated with the famous Mughal miniature style of painting based on the characterization of various ragas. Usually, there are no rules in a ragamala but ideally they should be ragas which are close to each other in their musical notes. The ragamallika is especially common in Carnatic music for both vocalists and instrumentalists. Though north Indian instrumentalists have also adapted this trend, it is less commonly presented by north Indian vocalists.

In vocal music, a style of singing originally of Persian origin, is often presented, characterized by rhythmic syllables which have no meaning, called **Tarana.** It is said that the tarana was pioneered by the great thirteenth-century Sufi, Amir Khusro. A vocal, rhythmic and melodic composition using phrases without meaning in Carnatic music is called **Tillana.**

At the end of the day, these are terms which it helps to be aware of and to keep at the back of your mind. What matters eventually is the music, the effect of music and the realization of the twelve notes of music.

CHAPTER 1

Ustad Abdul Halim Jaffer Khan

1929 -

Sitar maestro Abdul Halim Jaffer Khan is recognized as one of the leading representatives of the Indore Beenkar gharana, which also finds its roots in the musical legacies of the ustads Bande Ali Khan, Murad Khan and Babu Khan.

We had always heard the name of this great master from our father, but never got to meet him until he was presented with the Haafiz Ali Khan Award in 1993 in New Delhi, by the then President of India, Dr K.R. Narayanan. The other awardee that year was Dr Balamurali Krishna. Subsequently, we met Khan sahib on numerous occasions in Mumbai, and he has always received us with great love and warmth. He

Ustad Abdul Halim Jaffer Khan with Pandit Samta Prasad

is extremely fond of our father and also told us stories of our grandfather with whom he had exchanged many letters. His presence at a concert hall is inspiring for any performer because he is always very encouraging with his words.

In spite of the presence of so many great sitarists, Khan sahib managed to carve a niche for himself and created a style that was never before heard. He has taken festivals by storm wherever he has performed. He received the Sangeet Natak Academy award in 1987, and the Padmashri in 1970. His work speaks volumes for his skill and he is known for a distinctive style of playing that has been named the Jaffer Khani Baaj after him.

Through his innovation on the sitar, Khan sahib gives what the raga demands, and what the composition demands. His unique contribution and creative journey have made him the timeless artiste that he is today.

THE RECORDING

ALBUM: 75th Celebration Swara Sadhana Ustad Abdul Halim Jaffer Khan

RAGA: Zila Kafi

ACCOMPANIST: Sadashiv Pawar (tabla)
RELEASED BY: Navras Records (2004)

This is a very special recording that was made in 1968 in Jaipur and released on Khan sahib's 75th birthday. Khan sahib plays the fabulous Zila Kafi as a mainstream raga, though the raga is more commonly played as a lighter form of classical music. The 3rd and 7th notes of this raga are flat and the 2nd and 5th notes are aesthetically prominent. There is also a frugal usage of the sharp 3rd and 7th notes. The recording starts with the most romantic interpretation of this beautiful raga. Note by note, Khan sahib unfolds the most untold and pregnant phrases with his ecstatic touch to the sitar. A very brief jor follows the alaap.

The compositions are all based in teentaal. The first composition is a vilambit gat and some very interesting moments are captured in this track. Khan sahib improvises around the basic structure of the composition and one can sense his unique creativity. Some very momentous interactions between the sitar and tabla are captured along with some fast taans at the end.

Khan sahib then presents a beautiful composition in drut teentaal that captures the feel and essence of instrumental music. Splendid syllables of instrumental music are explored and the performance ends with a rapid firework crescendo with a tihai (a single unit played three times).

CHAPTER 2

Ustad Abdul Karim Khan

1872 - 1937

Abdul Karim Khan sahib is said to be the first north Indian artiste who was a court musician in Mysore. Born in Kirana, a village near Kurukshetra, he raised the banner of the Kirana gharana all over the Indian subcontinent.

Ustad Abdul Karim Khan received his musical legacy from his father Ustad Kale Khan and his uncle Ustad Abdulla Khan. In time, he was appointed as a court musician in the city of Baroda. He eventually settled in Miraj after living in Mumbai. In the early years of his life, he used to sing with his brother, Abdul Haq.

Khan sahib is credited with co-opting various south Indian ragas into north Indian music. He was perhaps the first north Indian artiste from that era who did a lot for the promotion of mutual understanding between Hindustani and Carnatic music. While at the Mysore court, he interacted with famous Carnatic masters who influenced his musical style and in 1913, he founded the Arya Sangeet Vidyalaya in Pune to spread the message of Indian classical music.

Abdul Karim Khan was a true genius and his approach and imagination inspired not just vocalists but also instrumentalists in the years to follow. His contribution to Hindustani classical music is unsurpassed. He passed on his musical legacy to his talented daughters, Hirabai Borodekar and Roshanara Begum.

His signature style was to emphasize notes in the upper octaves, which in time became a trend followed by many instrumentalists and vocalists. The appeal and power of Khan sahib's voice can truly move a listener to tears. It is said that the taaseer, the simplicity that his voice possessed, was never heard before him and, in fact, wasn't ever displayed by any other artiste after his passing away. He was a stalwart of his art form and a purist. The lightning gamaks and taans that he sang with effortless ease will remain an inspiration forever. Khan sahib died in 1937 at Miraj, during a concert tour of southern India.

THE RECORDING

ALBUM: Vintage 78 RPM Recordings Ustad Abdul Karim Khan
RELEASED BY: Saregama (1955)

This recording is only a trailer to the legacy of this brilliant legend and maestro. The atmosphere created is soothing and almost hypnotic. Raga Jogia is particularly mesmerizing as Khan sahib was famous for his rendition of the raga and 'Piya Ke Milan Ki Aas' is still sung by representatives of the Kirana gharana today.

1. Raga Lalit: 'Bhavda Yarda Yovan'

2. **Raga Gujri Todi:** 'Begun Gun Gaye'
3. **Raga Dev Gandhar:** 'Chandri Ka Hi Janu'
4. **Raga Bhimpalasi:** 'Prem Seva Sharan'
5. **Raga Patdeep:** 'Dhan Dhan Dhari'
6. **Raga Mishra Kafi:** 'Bawan Ram De Gayo Hori'
7. **Raga Marwa:** Tarana
8. **Raga Shudh Kalyan:** 'Monder Baje'
9. **Raga Mishra Jungla:** 'Ram Nagaria Mein Kaise Jaoon'
10. **Raga Shankara:** 'Aaj Suhag'
11. **Raga Basant:** 'Ab Main Ne Man Dekhe'
12. **Raga Jhinjhoti:** 'Piya Bin Nahin Awat'
13. **Raga Abhogi Kanhara:** 'Banara Rangila Mat'
14. **Raga Darbari Kanhara:** 'Jhankar Jhankva More'
15. **Raga Jogia:** 'Piya Ke Milan Ki Aas'
16. **Raga Anand Bhairavi:** 'Ugieh Ka Kanta'

Khan sahib's concept of music did not emphasize the technical but his approach was that of reverie, grace, emotion and appeal. He was perhaps unconventional in his time but his 'Shruti Samvad theory', which he advanced in collaboration with the British musicologist E. Clements, was in keeping with his pioneering musical approaches and techniques.

CHAPTER 3

Ustad Ahmed Jaan Thirakhwa

1892 – 1976

Ustad Ahmed Jaan Thirakhwa, the tabla wizard and patriarch, was born in Muradabad, Uttar Pradesh. He was born into a family of tabla players. His maternal grandfather, Baba Kalandar Baksh, and his brothers, Ilahi Baksh (Natoriwala), Boli Baksh, and Karim Baksh, were established tabla players in Muradabad. His maternal uncles Sher Khan, Fayaz Khan, Baswa Khan and Fazli Khan were also renowned tabla players and composers.

He was a simple man and spent most of his life in Mumbai. He accompanied great artistes like Ustad Alla Bande Khan, Ustad Rajab Ali Khan, Ustad Abdul Wahid Khan, Ustad Alladiya Khan, Ustad Faiyaz

Khan, Ustad Mustaque Hussain Khan, Pandit Bhasker Rao Bakhle, Pandit Achhan Maharaj, Srimati Gouharjan Bai, Srimati Malkajan Bai, Ustad Imdad Khan, Ustad Enayat Khan and Ustad Haafiz Ali Khan.

He mastered the different tabla gharanas and was famous for his art of improvisation. He was also one of the first tabla players to play solo. There was no tabla player who was not inspired by him or who did not follow him. He lived his life on his own terms and was a master of his craft and a true icon of the tabla. The nickname 'Thirakhwa' was affectionately given to him by his grandfather Ustad Kale Khan, who said that Ahmed Jaan's music was full of rapid movements whether he was singing or playing the tabla (hence 'Thirakhwa' from the Hindi word 'thirakhna', to dance). 'The world knows me less as Ahmed Jaan and more as Thirakhwa,' an amused Khan sahib once said.

This great legend of the tabla was awarded the Sangeet Natak Akademi Award in 1954 and the Padma Bhushan in 1970. After his death in 1976, his legacy has been carried forward by his sons, family and students.

THE RECORDING

ALBUM: Master Musicans of India: Ustad Ahmed Jaan Thirakhwa
TRACKS: Silsila, Gharana, Swaroop, Nikaas and Taleem
RELEASED BY: Saregama and Sangeet Natak Academy (2007)

This is a very unique recording where Ustad Ahmed Jaan Thirakhwa not only plays but also speaks and demonstrates many nuances of the tabla and gives a detailed background of tabla playing. Although the name of the lady interviewer is not mentioned, she too seems to be deeply engrossed in the music and the art of tabla playing.

1. Silsila: Ustad Ahmed Jaan Thirakhwa explains (with demonstration) the traditional system of presenting a tabla solo. The track is set to teentaal, and the artiste presents peshkars, farshbandis and chalans of Purab (Benaras and Farrukhabad). This is followed by some qaida ('rules') after which Khan sahib presents some thrilling relas followed by a gat and tukdas. He also recites some magnificent gats and tukdas and then goes back to presenting the relas. Again, he mentions the Farrukhabad Baant and presents some relas and qaida. One can hear his signature tirkits (rhythmic syllables).

2. Gharana: The Silsila is followed by an elaboration of the specialities of the four tabla gharanas — Delhi, Ajrara, Lucknow and Farrukhabad. Khan sahib describes each gharana, elaborating on its particular style. For instance, the Delhi gharana uses the 'two-finger playing technique', and the artiste recites the thekas and then plays them. This is followed by the elaboration of the qaida of the Ajrara school which is similar to the Delhi gharana in that it is also a two-finger technique of playing. After this, the Farrukhabad technique is described, where the artiste himself hails from, and finally the Lucknow school of playing is presented.

3. Swaroop: The artiste names the nineteen taals and recites and plays the thekas and bols with the appropriate laya of presentation.It is quite amusing to hear the interviewer make him recite and demonstrate just the thekas of more than ten taals. He very graciously obliges. He plays dhamaar (14 beats), jhoomra (14 beats), tilwada (16 beats), ada chautaal (14 beats), ektaal (12 beats), jhaptaal (10 beats) and a few more taals. He also speaks of the appropriate speed of presenting each taal.

4. Nikaas: The interviewer asks him which bols are particular to the tabla only and how they are different from dance bols. Khan sahib replies that this knowledge can only be passed on from guru to disciple. Instead he addresses the technique of playing different syllables (bols) of the tabla and compositions (bandishes). He demonstrates the instruments and speaks of the daaya and baaya, the use of the left and right hands. He then recites and plays some lightning qaidas and relas. Even though this recording was made at a later stage of his life, the strength and energy in his hands could put a twenty year old to shame.

5. Taleem: Ustad Ahmed Jaan Thirakhwa talks about his riyaz, the training during his formative years, and demonstrates some special compositions. He was nine or ten when he went to Mumbai. He describes how he left singing, left the sarangi and began to play the tabla which his heart was set upon. He speaks of his rigorous schedule of practice for twenty hours at a stretch. He mentions a term called 'chillah' which every classical musician, at least at one point of time, was familiar with. A chillah is a commitment to practising for a certain number of hours in a day within a specified period. It could be two hours or twenty-two hours. However, come what may, the artiste must stick to that timing for the chosen number of days or months. This great recording is summed up with Khan sahib presenting some more gats and tukdas and a thrilling chakradaar tihai.

CHAPTER 4

Ustad Ali Akbar Khan

1922 – 2009

In 1988, our father organized a six-day-long sarod festival at Kamani Hall in New Delhi. It was the first of its kind and the two of us secretly felt that the whole concept was a bit bizarre. Can you imagine Isaac Stern organizing a violin festival at his own expense only to present violinists from all over the country and dealing with all their demands? On December 28, 1988, our grandfather's death anniversary, Ali Akbar Khan sahib performed. This was the first time we met Ustad Ali Akbar Khan and heard him play. We were quite excited as he was our father's only sarod contemporary and their fathers, Ustad Allauddin Khan and Ustad Haafiz Ali Khan, had been taught by the same teacher,

Khan sahib with our family in San Jose, June 1996

Ustad Wazir Khan, though at different times. Ustad Wazir Khan was a direct descendant of Mian Tansen's family. Haafiz Ali Khan and Allauddin Khan are both representatives of the Senia gharana, but different names have been given to their schools over time.

We remember Khan sahib arriving at the venue, seated in the front seat of a Nissan. He was staying with the Bharatram family who were great patrons of his school of playing. That evening he played a raga called Durgeshwari, which was his own creation, followed by a ragamala in Bhairavi. We were to present him with a souvenir after the concert but were sent back home as it was past our bedtime!

In 1990, our parents took us to Kolkata to attend the Dover Lane Music Festival where our father was to give the concluding performance. The Dover Lane Music Festival is perhaps the oldest music festival in India and has been taking place for over fifty years. This historic festival is something of an entry ticket for any artiste into the world of Indian classical music. In its early years it used to take place at Vivekananda Park but from 1992, it has been held at Nazrul Mancha in Kolkata. That year the Dover Lane Music Festival had all the stars — Ravi Shankar, Ali Akbar Khan, Bhimsen Joshi, Vilayat Khan, Amjad Ali Khan, Bismillah Khan, Birju Maharaj and many others.

We went backstage and met Ali Akbar Khan sahib, who asked us if we were playing too. He played Raga Medhavi (his own creation), Chayanat and Bhairavi that day. His older son Ashish Khan assisted him on the sarod. We sat next to his wife and sons who were visiting Kolkata at that time from the US. After this meeting, we attended a few other concerts of Khan sahib's in New Delhi and Kolkata but never really got to know him well. We met him once again in 1996 when he came for our concert in San Jose. During the intermission, he came backstage and spent some very memorable moments with our family. After the concert, he blessed us and said that he was very happy to have heard us play. Khan sahib also expressed his disapproval about a controversy that one of his senior students, Sharan Rani, had started in newspapers earlier that year regarding the origin of the sarod. This was a baseless controversy that claimed that the sarod existed from 500 BC though there are no historical or musical facts to prove this. In fact, the sarod originated in Afghanistan from an Afghan folk instrument called the rabab. In time, it was modified in India by Ghulam Ali Khan Bangash (who happens to be one of our forefathers). In fact, in the inlay of most of Khan sahib's LPs, this was always mentioned.

Amaan also met Khan sahib with our father at his school of music in California in 1998. The last time we heard Khan sahib play was once again at the Dover Lane Music Festival in 2002 where he played a fabulous Gunji Kanhara and ragamala.

It was indeed a sad moment for the world of music when Khan sahib passed away in San Rafael in California on June 18, 2009. We gave our condolences to his family in California a few days later. We are very fortunate to have met him and received his blessings. He has left behind a legacy that is priceless. His teachings, his musical genius and his calibre are unparalleled. We pray for his family, and as sarod players we will miss him no end.

THE RECORDING

ALBUM: Artistic Sound of Sarod

RAGAS: Basant Mukhari and Jogia

ACCOMPANISTS: Swapan Chaudhuri (tabla), Shefali Nag and Daniel Paul Karp (tanpura)

RELEASED BY: Chhanda Dhara (1985)

1. Raga Basant Mukhari: Raga Basant Mukhari is one of the most haunting morning ragas. The rendering of this raga vividly creates passion, feeling and depth. The framework of the notes is as follows:

ASCENDING: Sa re Ga Ma Pa dha ni
DESCENDING: Sa ni dha Pa Ma Ga re

The composition begins with the traditional alaap, with which the raga is introduced to its renderer and listener. This alaap is testimony to Khan sahib's genius as it flows like poetry with the ideal punctuations. The raga is slowly unfolded with long slides and glides, which is one of the most distinctive and beautiful features of the sarod.

2. Raga Jogia: The next raga is Jogia, a raga that is actually very popular with vocalists rather than instrumentalists. The notes are:

ASCENDING: Sa re Ma Pa dha
DESCENDING: Sa ni dha Pa Ma Ga re

The notes are in common with Basant Mukhari but there is a unique difference in the structure, flavour and character of Jogia. Jogia is usually performed as a concluding piece at concerts, like Raga Bhairavi. Khan sahib plays two compositions, one in jhaptaal and the other in teentaal. A lot of sellable work and layakari dominate the jhaptaal section with the tabla improvising constantly in between the sarod improvisations. The tabla accompaniment is provided by Swapan Chaudhuri who has had a phenomenal musical understanding with Khan sahib for many years. The drut composition in teentaal is a very typical composition of Khan sahib's school of sarod playing with some breathtaking rhythmic patterns.

CHAPTER 5

Ustad Amir Khan

1912 - 1974

Ustad Amir Khan is undoubtedly one of the greatest vocalists that India has ever seen. He was the musician's musician. A purist by nature, he never compromised on his approach or his aesthetics throughout his musical journey. He created a style that was unique and was worshipped with devotion by music lovers. Amir Khan was a pioneer in his approach to khayal singing, which influenced most of the singers of his time. Incorporating the styles of Abdul Waheed Khan, Rajab Ali Khan and Aman Ali Khan, Ustad Amir Khan developed his own style of singing under the Indore gharana.

Born in 1912, he was the son of Ustad Shahmir Khan, a noted sarangi

and been player in Indore. His father was a court musician for the Holkars, while his grandfather had been a singer at the court of Bahadur Shah Zafar. Amir Khan received extensive training in singing from his father, including the important and difficult technique of Khand-Meru, which is the knowledge of the 5040 taans, or combinations and permutations possible in a musical scale. Immense practice in this technique gave Amir Khan's singing its polished repertoire of fantastically devious taans. The Government of India awarded him the Sangeet Natak Akademi Award in 1967 and he was decorated with the Padma Bhushan in 1971.

Besides singing in concerts, Amir Khan also sang for the Indian film industry, including some timeless movies like *Baiju Bawra*, *Kshudhita Pashan*, *Shabaab* and *Jhanak Jhanak Payal Baaje*. On the personal front, Khan sahib's first marriage was to the sister of Ustad Vilayat Khan. He died a premature death in an unfortunate car accident in Kolkata in 1974.

THE RECORDING

ALBUM: Ustad Amir Khan
RAGAS: Raga Marwa and Raga Darbari Kanhara
ACCOMPANISTS: Unknown
RELEASED BY: Saregama (1960)

1. Raga Marwa: Ustad Amir Khan and this particular raga seem inseparable from one another. He was the exemplar of how Raga Marwa should be handled and presented. In this recording, Khan sahib gives the raga its true feel and character. The frugal use of Sa, a typical feature of Raga Marwa, is done most appropriately. The sargams and some powerful fast taans are demonstrated. Khan sahib has a very interesting pattern of using sargams that go back and forth from the upper notes to the counter lower notes. Two compositions are sung, one in jhoomrataal called 'Piya Mohe Aanat Des' and the second in a medium tempo composition set to teentaal called 'Guru Bin Gyaan Na Pawe'.

2. Raga Darbari Kanhara: Khan sahib has done complete justice to the majestic raga of Mian Tansen in this rendition. He begins with a very slow and gradual movement of Darbari Kanhara with the phenomenal use of the mandra saptak, which is the octave below the madhya saptak. The notes of this octave are sung or played in a low deep tone. The signature Amir Khan taans and sargams take over as the track progresses. The two compositions sung are 'Eri Birari' in jhoomra and a fast composition in teentaal called 'Kin Bairan Kan Bhare'.

Interestingly, the tanpuras in this track are tuned with a prominent shuddha Ni, whereas Darbari does not have that note. One of Khan sahib's unique characteristics was to switch ragas rapidly, barely stopping for a moment, so his tanpura would be tuned to the first raga with which he began his concert, or in this case, recording.

CHAPTER 6

Ustad Amjad Ali Khan

1945 –

What can you say about an icon whose very name means music to you? What do you write about a man for whom the world is music and music is the world? For us, the twelve letters in his name are the twelve notes of music. A great son of a great guru and father, Ustad Haafiz Ali Khan, he is an example of pioneering techniques and breathing a new voice, new life and new meaning into sarod playing and into Indian classical music.

When you hear Amjad Ali Khan sahib today, you of course hear him, but you also hear the voices of Abdul Karim Khan and Bade Ghulam Ali Khan, the strings of Ustad Haafiz Ali Khan and Ustad

Enayet Khan. This artiste has analyzed, observed and filtered music to his advantage from all these greats. The concept of compositions for instrumental music took a historic turn with his entry into the world of Indian classical music. Ragas like Saraswati, Bhoopali, Hansdhwani and Abhogi were heard on his sarod, which had never been attempted by any sarod player. He made it look easy and sound easy, where it wasn't. He is solely responsible for making the sarod sing. His greatest contribution has been the evolution of the Ekehra taans on the sarod, which are played on a single note and with a single stroke. Today, the sarod has become synonymous with the name Amjad Ali Khan.

A purist at heart, he has collaborated with diverse artistes and orchestras. He has been a complete trendsetter; so much so that we have sometimes come across sarod players who, apart from the musical inspiration, walk like him, talk like him and want to just be him. Today, most sarod players and sarod lovers have his music in their playlist or music collections. There isn't a single young sarod player today who has not been inspired by him or who doesn't follow him, even though they may not admit it.

He has been a loner in his field and has had a very private and lonely journey with no musical partnerships in the world of Indian classical music.

An artiste who has set standards in his own way with dignity, sophistication and musical genius, we know him as a timeless guru, a doting father and a beautiful human being. He is a monumental icon of

Indian classical music in our time and it is hard to say whether he chose the sarod or the sarod chose him.

THE RECORDING

ALBUM: Guldasta (A bouquet of flowers)
ARTISTE: Ustad Amjad Ali Khan, sarod
RAGAS: Shiva Ranjini, Hansdhwani, Zila Kafi, Anandi, Shiv Kalyan, Saraswati and Bhairavi
ACCOMPANISTS: Jayanta Bose and Shamim Ahmad (tabla)
RELEASED BY: Saregama (1983)

It is quite difficult to choose one great album of your own guru and father. As sentimental as it may sound, the truth remains that we love all his recordings released till date. However, from a historical point of view, we decided to talk about *Guldasta*, an album that was ahead of its time for many reasons.

When *Guldasta* was released in 1983, it was quite a controversial album. That was an era of classical music when improvisations were at its peak. The same raga could go on for three hours! Needless to say, after the first hour, it was all repetition. Our grandfather Ustad Haafiz Ali Khan would often say, 'Let's not operate a raga.' In this album, Abba decided to fight against the current, and instead of recording one long raga or two ragas (at that time on either side of an LP, Side A and Side B), he decided to record nine short ragas. The other unusual feature was the titles he used, which were quite unconventional back in the eighties when the rules of purity and tradition in classical music were extremely important. These days, an album of this nature is a marketing bliss for music labels as the demand today is for short pieces!

The album opens with the artiste addressing the audience

in Urdu, which again was a very new element as most albums opened directly with the music. Musically, this was the first album in the history of Indian classical music where a listener heard Raga Hansdhwani and Saraswati on the sarod. This was a pioneering phenomenon as no sarod player had ever attempted these ragas. The compositions quickly became popular and, in fact, each composition captures the raga beautifully. The single note and single stroke ekehra taans started by Ustad Amjad Ali Khan on the sarod are heard in their most developed form. There is also an interesting variety of taals played in this album.

A few more ragas (Darbari Kanhara, Lalita Dhwani, Mishra Khamaj and Behag) were in the LP but did not make it to the CD due to the time constraints. This is a recording that captures the maestro's innovative and timeless journey into the world of music.

1. Recalling our love

Based on Raga Shiva Ranjini set to dadra (6 beats)

This is a Carnatic raga and is played here like a song full of depth, pathos and melancholy. The composition itself can move a listener to tears.

2. I feel your presence

Based on Raga Hansdhwani set to teentaal (16 beats)

One of the most popular south Indian ragas, this raga has the most pleasant effect on any listener. It is recorded on the sarod for the first time here.

3. Rainbows adorn you

Based on Raga Zila Kafi set to chachar (14 beats)

A raga that is closely associated with the colourful festival of Holi, this is a most authentic interpretation of the vocal nuances of Zila Kafi, a raga that is a bible for every vocalist, especially thumri singers. As love adds colour to life, Zila Kafi adds the flavour of romance to this album. Like a vocalist, the artiste gives room to the tabla accompanists for a laggi at the end of the track.

4. Wish you were here

Based on Raga Anandi set to teentaal (16 beats)

The traditional Anandi Kalyan played here is a very popular vocal composition which is often sung by artistes. Several vocal elements and styles are adapted in this performance. The prominent sequence 'Ga Ma Dha Pa Re' shines through and the antara is any vocalist's envy.

5. In search of you

Based on Raga Shiv Kalyan set to rupaktaal (7 beats)

Also known as Raga Janasammohini in the south, Shiv Kalyan was a popular raga among the Patiala gharana of singers. A beautiful raga played in a magical composition in 7 beats' time cycle. The composition complements the rhythmic cycle itself. A genius creation from a genius mind!

6. I feel lonely

Based on Raga Saraswati set to ektaal (12 beats)

This was the first time that Raga Saraswati was recorded on the sarod. It is one of the most complex ragas to play on the sarod. This unique composition is set to 12 beats and the sum is dramatically on Re (the 2nd note) as demanded by the raga structure. Some flawless taans and patterns are played effortlessly with deep innovations.

7. Each dawn renews our dream

Based on Raga Bhairavi set to teentaal (16 beats and dadra (6 beats)

The evergreen raga, the dessert of the raga dinner party! Commonly called Sada Suhaagan due to the usage of all the twelve notes, the first composition is one of the most popular ones by the maestro and has audiences humming along whenever he performs it. The track concludes with a lighter version of Bhairavi played in dadra. A climax that spiritually elevates a listener!

CHAPTER 7

Dr Balamurali Krishna

1930 –

Balamurali Krishna is a highly acclaimed Carnatic vocalist whose voice captures emotion and spiritual devotion in every musical note. A multifaceted artiste, he can also play the violin, the viola, the mridangam and the kanjira in the most effortless manner. His emphasis has always been on the sacredness of each note and the accuracy of the raga. He values the element of voice culture no end. He believes in the accuracy of every note, be it in Indian classical music from the north or the south. His music was also very closely connected to and inspired by his spiritual faith. He said, 'I compose whenever the inspiration comes to me, particularly when I visit temples.'

Mangalampalli Balamurali Krishna was born in a small village called Sankaraguptam in Andhra Pradesh. He began his musical training at a very tender age and gave his first concert when he was just eight. He learned under Parupalli Ramakrishnaiah Pantulu of Vijayawada, a pure classicist and a strict disciplinarian.

For many years, he was the principal of the Government Music College at Vijayawada and also a producer of music in both Vijayawada and Madras for All India Radio.

Dr Balamurali Krishna has the honour of being the state musician of both Tamil Nadu and Andhra Pradesh and also the Asthana Vidwan of Tirumala Tirupati Devasthanam. He is also a recipient of the Padmashri, Padma Bhushan and Padma Vibhushan. His duets with Bhimsen Joshi have been a pioneering presentation of north and south Indian music coming together, more so because they come from two legendary vocalists. As a playback singer for the south Indian film industry, he received a national award for 'best playback singer' for his involvement in the film *Hamsageeth* and for 'best music director' for the film *Madhvacharya*.

We were very fortunate to meet Dr Balamurali Krishna quite a number of times, the first being in 1993 when he received the Haafiz Ali Khan Award in New Delhi at the Siri Fort Auditorium from the then Vice-president of India, Dr K.R. Narayanan. After this, we heard him in Paris when he performed after our father at UNESCO on the occasion of Mahatma Gandhi's 125th birth anniversary. We were very fortunate to hear him and Abba performing in New Delhi together once again for Mahatma Gandhi's 125th birth anniversary the same year in New Delhi. Interestingly, the duet was between the sarod and the viola, rather than vocal. His command over the viola shows the mark of true genius. We also heard a memorable duet between Dr Balamurali Krishna and Pandit Hari Prasad Chaurasia in New Delhi in 1994 for the Rajiv Gandhi Foundation. He made a humorous announcement in praise of Hari Prasad Chaurasia, saying that he was only Bala that day and that Hari Prasad Chaurasia had taken the 'Murali' away! Warm, always pleasant and a true doyen of his industry, here is a man who is today a symbol of Carnatic music.

THE RECORDING

ALBUM: Maestro's Choice

Maestro's Choice is a series of recordings that was released in the nineties, each album dedicated to one artiste, where the artistes selected the ragas themselves.

RAGAS: Purvikalyani, Abhogi, Kanada, Lavangi, Behag

ACCOMPANISTS: Annavarapu Ramaswamy (violin), Mahadevu Laxminarayana Raju (mridangam), T.H. Subashchandran (ghatam), Basavaraju V. Balasai (flute)

RELEASED BY: Music Today (1991)

1. Raga Purvikalyani: Needaya Rada (tala adi)
The artiste mentions in the inlay that he had sung this song in the Kanakadurga temple in Vijayawada. It was a spontaneous creation by this great virtuoso.The word 'Hari' alone resonates for the first few minutes.

2. Raga Abhogi: Vegamay (tala adi)
A self-composed piece by the artiste in Raga Abhogi, a raga that was very commonly performed at one point of time by many north Indian classical musicians as well. The piece was conceived when Balamurali Krishna visited Pandharpur with his guru.

3. Raga Kanada: Brihadeesvara (tala rupakam)
This track was thought of by the artiste when he visited Thanjavur. Thanjavur was the cultural centre of the country in 1790 and became prominent during the reign of the Chola kings, who made it their capital. It is a town that has contributed greatly to Carnatic music and dance.

4. Raga Lavangi: Omkara (tala adi)
Spirituality and music in India have gone hand in hand right from the Vedic times. Hence is it understandable that most of

the tracks in this recording have been invoked, created and thought of in a spiritual moment by the artiste. Lavangi is a raga conjured up by the great singer himself and happens to be one of his favourites. The inspiration for this piece came from Vedic chants and the raga was conceptualized with only three or four notes, as in the Vedic chants.

5. Raga Behag: Tillana (tala adi)

As a tribute to the saint musician Thyagaraja, Balamurali Krishna concludes this great album with a tillana in Raga Behag. The ghatam accompaniment has been done by T.H. Subashchandran who is the younger brother of T.H. Vinayak Ram. We have had the honour of performing with both the genius brothers on numerous occasions.

CHAPTER 8

Ustad Bade Ghulam Ali Khan

1902 – 1968

One of the first Indian classical vocalists to sing in a commercial Hindi film (K. Asif's *Mughal-e-Azam* in 1960), Bade Ghulam Ali Khan endeared himself to a wide audience with his amazingly honey-sweet voice. This father figure of Indian vocal music was born in Kasur, now in Pakistani Punjab. Ustad Bade Ghulam Ali Khan was the torchbearer of the celebrated Patiala school of music, which he had established. He died in 1968 at the relatively young age of 66. The ustad learned sarangi and vocal from his paternal uncle Kale Khan, who was a great singer himself, and later trained under his father Ali Baksh Khan. He also took vocal lessons from Baba Shinde Khan.

His musical genius, impressive stage presence and towering personality all added up to make him a monumental icon of his craft. Arriving on the music scene in the mid-thirties, he came and conquered immediately. He became an obsession with listeners and was imitated by amateurs and vocalists alike. His canvas was unique and his usage of notes and embellishments was rhapsody at its best, summed up best by the single word 'electrifying'.

Khan sahib began the trend of singing to very complex taals like ada chataal and many other complicated taals which are somewhat unusual in vocal music, something that has been followed by other exponents of the Patiala gharana. His legacy was continued by his disciples, his son Munawar Ali Khan and his grandsons. The Patiala gharana has today become a name that most vocalists like to be associated with. Our father recalls sharing some magical moments with Khan sahib in Kolkata and at various festivals all over India, discussing work, music and life.

THE RECORDING

ALBUM: Ustad Bade Ghulam Ali Khan
RAGAS: Gujri Todi, Desi Todi, Bhimpalasi, Kamod, Pahadi, Kedar, Jaijaiwanti, Darbari Kanhara, Adana, Malkauns and Paraj
RELEASED BY: Saregama (1997)

1. Gujri Todi: 'Bhori Bhai'
This electrifying piece tells the listener what the great singer was all about, within the first few moments of the track. This is also the song that was picked up by music director A.R. Rahman for the film *Delhi 6* where the original voice of the ustad was used along with Shreya Ghoshal's voice. Hence, his association with the film industry continues even after he is no more.

2. Desi Todi: 'Manva Larje'
Words are not enough to describe Khan sahib's magical interpretation of the rare raga Desi Todi. The asar (impact) on the listener is beyond description. The track is full of lightning taans of intensely complex patterns.

3. Raga Bhimpalasi: 'Be Gun Kahe'
The beauty of this evergreen afternoon raga lies in its simplicity. This track flows as smoothly as a river and conjures up a world without worries. Khan sahib repeats his usual magic and accentuations.

4. Raga Kamod: 'Chhand De Mora'
Raga Kamod is presented here with Khan sahib's genius, only to make it a landmark track. The rendering of thumris and other lighter classical pieces as well as folk music (like the following track in Pahadi) are very subjective and personal. A teacher may teach you the essence, but the eventual interpretation is individual.

5. Raga Pahadi: 'Hari Om Tatsat'
This rendition of Pahadi, the Himachal Pradesh folk tune, by Khan sahib grew to become a household favourite. One can sense the artiste's journey with his interpretation of folk music. A winner track!

6. Raga Kedar: 'Naveli Naar'
The composition is in ektaal. The traditional use of the komal nishad, the 6th note, which is a key element in this raga and a rather subtle one at that, is done very gracefully. The signature firework taans are heard in this track, along with the inspiring notes of Kedar.

7. Raga Jaijaiwanti: 'Binati Ka Kariye'
A favourite among vocalists then and now, this raga has

been invoked beautifully by Khan sahib in this album. The prominent phrase 'Ni Sa Dha ni Re' flows beautifully.

8. Raga Darbari: 'Bhaj Re Har Naam'

This raga was created by the great Tansen in the fifteenth century, and is a bible for every musician. Khan sahib's imagination makes this raga an even greater celebration of music.

9. Raga Adana: 'Jaisi Karini Vaisi Bharini'

The words of this song interestingly mean 'you pay for your actions'! This raga is sung in the uttarang (upper octave), which is a unique and prominent feature of Raga Adana, and this composition is an electrifying testimony to Khan sahib's musical genius.

10. Raga Malkauns: 'Mandir Dekh Dare'

Khan sahib does great justice to Malkauns, going right up to the higher octaves.

11. Raga Paraj: 'Latak Ma'

A fitting conclusion to this masterpiece of an album, Paraj is a springtime raga, often confused with Raga Basant by many vocalists and instrumentalists.

CHAPTER 9

Begum Akhtar

1914 - 1974

India's original singing diva, Begum Akhtar carried with her a grace and aura that was every singer's envy. Often addressed as 'Mallika', queen of music, her aesthetics were uncanny and she could bring the house down effortlessly.

Born on October 7, 1914, Begum Akhtar trained under Ustad Abdul Waheed Khan of the Kirana school and Ustad Ata Mohamed Khan of the Patiala school. She brought dignity and sophistication to what was derogatorily termed as light music, compromising ghazals, thumri and dadra. She won a zillion hearts over the Indian subcontinent and was earlier known to her admirers as Akhtari Bai

Faizabadi (named after the city of Faizabad). Her voice was described as honeyed melancholy.

THE RECORDING

ALBUM: The Gramaphone Eka, Begum Akhtar
RELEASED BY: Saregama

Begum Akhtar presents a few ghazals in this recording. One must understand that it's only the text, the lyrics that create a song, a ghazal or a qawwali. Basically, all music is based on the same twelve notes in the world. Hence, a ghazal can have all the gravity and depth that we have in this recording or on the other hand, one can make it cheap, vulgar and commercial to swell up sales.

In this recording, Begum Akhtar sings the most soulful tracks charged with intense romantic appeal. Each of the following songs exemplifies the magic and talent that she possessed.

1. **Kafi Thumri**
2. **Thumri (Mishra Tilak Kamod)**
3. **Dadra:** 'Zara Dhire'
4. **Thumri:** 'Akhiyan Neend'
5. **Thumri:** 'Nandiya Kahe'
6. 'Aaye Mohabbat'
7. 'Deewana Banana'
8. 'Ulti Ho'
9. 'Barsan Lagin'
10. 'Nihure Nihure'
11. 'Hamari Kahin'
12. 'Hamari Atariya'

The first track itself describes her genius and her musicianship. Be it the Kafi thumri or the thumri in Mishra Tilak Kamod (Track 2), her interpretations are genius! All the tracks have the most sublime creativity and imagination. The thumri in Track 5 based on Raga Tilang uses both komal and shuddha Ni. She was truly the all-time queen of Indian classical music.

CHAPTER 10

Pandit Bhimsen Joshi

1922 -

Supremely melodic patterns, a voice full of ardour and warmth, and perfect proportion and balance in the gradual unfolding of a raga — this is Pandit Bhimsen Joshi and the basis of his musical excellence.

The moment one thinks of buying a Hindustani vocal CD, Bhimsen Joshi is the name that springs to most minds. His name is synonymous with vocal music, and the love, admiration and ardent fan following that this legend has earned over the years remains unparalleled. Having run away from home to pursue a musical career, he had to face an initial struggle to achieve his dream. Riding on the crest of popularity for several decades now, he finally received the highest civilian award of India, the Bharat Ratna, in 2008.

Pandit Bhimsen Joshi's journey as a youngster was full of struggle. As a child, a recording of Ustad Abdul Karim Khan sahib had a huge impact on him and he went in search of a guru across cities in India, including Gwalior. In fact, he always makes it a point to mention that he learned Ragas Marwa and Puriya from Ustad Haafiz Ali Khan in Gwalior in the 1930s. Finally, Panditji started learning from Pandit Sawai Gandharva in the traditional guru-shishya style. In time, Panditji became the symbol and perhaps the ambassador of his school of singing.

Panditji has shared a wonderful relationship with our father. We have met him on several occasions since 1988, the most memorable

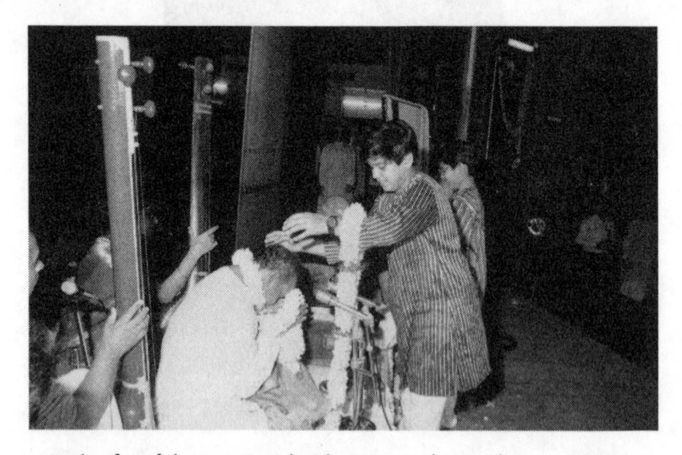

Both of us felicitate Pandit Bhimsen Joshi in Chennai, 1989

exposure being during his concert at our residence in 1993 on our father's birthday. He very affectionately got us shrikhand from Pune when he came to our home. We heard him live at a public concert for the first time at the Dover Lane Music Festival in 1990, when he sang Raga Darbari Kanhara before Ustad Vilayat Khan took the stage.

When we were young, our father used to take us to attend the Sawai Gandharva Music Festival, which Panditji has been organizing in Pune for the past two decades. We were made to sit behind our father on stage, and just observe his interaction with the audience which was made up of several thousand people even in the wee hours of the morning. In recent years we have been fortunate to have played solo at this music festival, and Panditji, even at this age, has blessed our performances with his presence. A true veteran of our cultural legacy, Bhimsen Joshi is indeed the reigning king of the Kirana gharana.

THE RECORDING

ALBUM: Pandit Bhimsen Joshi, Vocal
RAGAS: Komal Rishabh Asawari and Marwa
ACCOMPANISTS: Shripad Nageshkar
RELEASED BY: Saregama (1968)

1. Raga Komal Rishab Asawari: Vilambit ektaal (12 beats) 'Sab Mera Wohi Sakal Jagat Ko'
Komal Rishab Asawari is a very rare raga, but Panditji sings it effortlessly. He establishes the very strong character and flavour of the raga in no time. The typical phrases of 're Ma Pa dha' and 'Ma Pa dha Sa' are delivered in the most refined manner. A very gradual improvisation takes place, showing the khayal style typical of Bhimsen Joshi.

2. Raga Komal Rishab Asawari: Drut teentaal (16 beats) 'Main To Tumro Daas'
A very beautiful composition in teentaal; equally beautiful are the lyrics of the song that literally mean 'O lord, I am your servant.' Some ecstatic gamaks (embellishments) are heard in this track.

3. Raga Marwa: Vilambit ektaal (12 beats) 'Ab Mil Aaye Apne Piya Ke'

4. Raga Marwa: Drut teentaal (16 beats) 'Bangri Mori Murak Gai Chhand'
Raga Marwa has been a personal favourite of Bhimsen Joshi for years. The use of the note Sa in this raga is frugal. The raga is very heavy and creates pathos and a great amount of feeling among listeners.

CHAPTER 12

Ustad Bismillah Khan

1916 – 2006

The shehnai and Ustad Bismillah Khan are synonymous. It's as if Khan sahib was sent to the earth by the Almighty just to give the shehnai a place in mainstream classical music. He truly achieved this, and how!

Born in Dumraon, Bihar, in 1916, Bismillah Khan sahib hailed from a family of court musicians. He shifted to Benaras to train under his maternal uncle Ustad Ali Baksh, a great shehnai player of the Vishwanath Temple. He spent most of his life in this holy city leading the life of a pious Muslim, but playing with equal devotion at Hindu shrines, upholding the truly secular tradition of Indian classical music. Having

first brought the instrument to the centrestage at the All India Music Conference in Calcutta in 1937, Bismillah Khan continued to regale audiences all over India at prestigious music conferences and gatherings for over seven decades.

Bismillah Khan sahib was a man who led a life of simplicity and he lived it on his own terms. He generously supported his large joint family and it was indeed sad to see the financial crisis that he went through in the twilight of his career, which became so public. We were very fortunate that he released our collaboration album with cellist Matthew Barley, *Strings Attached*, at Science City in Kolkata, before his jugalbandi performance with our father in December 2003. Interestingly, Bismillah Khan is the only artiste to have played a duet with both the sitar icons, Ustad Vilayat Khan and Pandit Ravi Shankar.

He has received several national awards, from the Bharat Ratna to the Padma Shri, and played in 1947 at India's Independence and also in 1950 at the first Republic Day celebrations. His recital telecast on Doordarshan every Independence Day became a part of India's musical heritage.

We first met Khan sahib in Chennai in 1988, when he had come to receive the Haafiz Ali Khan Award at Rani Sethai Auditorium. He gave a very touching speech about our grandfather. We heard him play that same year at Sapru House, New Delhi. There is a lingering memory of Kathak danseuse Uma Sharma sitting backstage and tapping her feet impatiently, her ghungrus jingling to the rhythm. She was scheduled to perform after Khan sahib and was not too happy about the long wait. We were seeing the traits of the trade early in life! We again met Khan sahib more recently when he performed two duets with our father in New Delhi and in Kolkata in 2003.

Bismillah Khan continued to play until the very end when he passed away in Varanasi at the age of ninety. His death has been a great loss to the music world and marks the end of a glorious chapter in the shehnai tradition. He was a true performer and a great artiste. He knew what the audience wanted and how to create magic. His simple aura, his sense of humour and his god-fearing persona made him one of the most endearing personalities the music world has ever seen.

THE RECORDING

ALBUM: Vintage 78 RPM Records Ustad Bismillah Khan

RAGAS: Lalit, Todi, Ahir Bhairav, Jaunpuri, Shudh Sarang, Multani, Hansnarayani, Maru Behag, Tilak Kamod, Kedar, Raagmala, Dadra, Kajri, Basant Bahar, Bageshwari, Malkauns, Pahadi, Title Music Kajri, Bihag (Tera Sur aur Mera Geet), Jaijaiwanti (Jiwan Mein Piya Tera Saath Rahe), Bhairavi (Dil Ka Khilauna Haay Toot Gaya)

RELEASED BY: Saregama (2007)

1. Raga Lalit: The breathtaking Lalit uses both the 4th notes and creates a frenzy in the minds of listeners. It is played effortlessly by the shehnai titan.

2. Raga Todi: This timeless raga has never sounded better. A very traditional composition is played here, almost vocal in its interpretation. The beauty of Khan sahib's approach is its simplicity that imperceptibly takes a turn for the divine.

3. Raga Ahir Bhairav: This raga is played in a very relaxed manner by Khan sahib. The prominent combination of notes 'ni Sa Dha ni re' is frequented in the composition. Some wonderful elements of the shehnai are explored in this track.

4. Raga Jaunpuri: This pathbreaking morning raga is very challenging and has the same notes as Darbari Kanhara. It is just the distinct movement that gives it its special identity. Khan sahib does full justice to the raga and its approach. This is also a raga that is seldom attempted by instrumentalists as its framework is very challenging.

5. Raga Shudh Sarang: A legendary afternoon raga, Shudh Sarang uses both flat and sharp versions of the 4th note, as is typical of the Sarang family of ragas. The 4th note or madhyam is used individually in its sharp and flat forms, but may also be used together in an aesthetic way.

6. Raga Multani: The composition is based in ektaal. Multani is an early evening raga that is hardly performed now as concerts are usually held in the late evening. The promiment phrase of this raga is the combination of notes 'ma ga re Sa'.

7. Raga Hansnarayani: A rarely heard raga, this is perhaps its only recorded version. The notes are very close to Puriya Dhanashri, with the Dha (6th note) omitted.

8. Raga Maru Behag: Khan sahib plays a very traditional composition in Maru Behag. He adds embellishments on his shehnai that almost sound vocal, with the utmost ease and depth of feeling.

9. Raga Tilak Kamod: The composition is actually based on Raga Bihari, but the label describes it as Raga Tilak Kamod, a very close cousin. The use of the komal Ni in the second part indicates that it is indeed Bihari, though all other movements are very close to Tilak Kamod.

10. Raga Kedar (duet with Ustad Abdul Halim Jaffer Khan) Part 1: Perhaps one of Khan sahib's earlier duets, he collaborates with the well-known sitarist in a fabulous rendition of Kedar. It is a magical piece, where they are in complete sync with each other.

11. Raga Kedar (duet with Ustad Abdul Halim Jaffer Khan) Part 2: The duet continues to a crescendo. The jhala is established skilfully by both the maestros on sitar and shehnai. A truly memorable piece.

12. Ragamala (Sur Malhar, Bageshwari and Chandra Kauns) with Ustad Amir Khan*: This is a very unique track with the rather unusual combination of Bismillah Khan sahib on the shehnai with the great Ustad Amir Khan on vocal. A collector's bliss!

13. Dadra*

14. Kajri*

15. Raga Basant Bahar: The haunting combination of ragas Basant and Bahar come together. The beauty lies in playing it as one entity. A very challenging raga for instrumentalists, this track makes the shehnai take the shape of a vocalist in Khan sahib's rendition.

16. Raga Bageshwari: The evergreen Raga Bageshwari

is played with amazing authority by Khan sahib and is almost vocal in its interpretation.

17. Raga Malkauns: Here, Khan sahib plays a very popular shehnai composition that is often played at weddings and in Indian films.

18. Raga Pahadi*

19. Title Music Kajri*

21. Raga Bihag: 'Tera Sur aur Mera Geet'*

22. Raga Jaijaiwanti: 'Jiwan Mein Piya Tera Saath Rahe'*

23. Raga Bhairavi: 'Dil Ka Khilauna Haay Toot Gaya'*

* In the year 1959, Bismillah Khan sahib played these tunes in the Hindi film *Goonj Uthi Shenai*, produced by Prakash Pictures and directed by Vijay Bhatt. The music director was Vasant Desai. This gave an enormous boost to the shehnai at that point of time.

CHAPTER 12

D.K. Pattammal

1919 - 2009

For Damal Krishnaswamy Dikshitar Pattammal, music was always the obvious choice. She showed an intense interest in music from the age of five and took audiences by storm when she gave her first public performance when she was just eight. She came from an orthodox brahmin family in Kancheepuram, Tamil Nadu, where it was not easy for a girl to learn music, yet she grew to become a highly acclaimed vocalist.

She was very fortunate to have learnt from some of the greatest stalwarts like Ambi Dikshitar, who was the great-grandson of Muthuswami

Dikshitar (one of the trinities of south Indian music) and his disciple T.L. Venkatrama Iyer, Narasimhalu Naidu, Professor P. Sambamoorthy and others. Due to her rich musical tutelage, she was known to have one of the greatest repertoires of both old and new compositions. D.K. Pattammal, M.S. Subbulakshmi and M.L. Vasanthakumari were together known as the female trinity of Carnatic music.

Pattammal had a spiritual flair, a colourful vision and musicianship of the highest calibre. She was a queen in her interpretation of Muthuswami Dikshitar's compositions. In fact, many of his songs were popularized by Pattammal. Thyagaraja and Shyama Shastri's compositions were also her trump cards and always left the listener mesmerized. She learnt and popularized many compositions of Papanasam Sivan, besides popularizing compositions of many composers such as Subramanya Bharathi, Suddhananda Bharathi and other Carnatic legends. She had her unique style of articulation, diction and the rendering of pallavis in intricate talas.

She has been a pioneer in her lifetime. From being one of the first housewives to sing in a concert hall, she was the first female vocalist to sing ragam tanam pallavi in concerts and also one of the earliest singers from south India to sing in films. She was bestowed with the title 'Gana Saraswathi' by the great Tiger Varadachariar, Sangeetha Kalanidhi from the Madras Music Academy, the Fellowship of the Sangeet Natak Academy, the Haafiz Ali Khan Award in 1990 and the Padma Vibhushan in 1998.

We are very honoured to have met this great queen of vocal music. The first time we met her was in Chennai; it was December 1993 when she had come for our debut concert at Narada Gana Sabha. After this, we met her yet again at Narada Gana Sabha in 1995 during our father's fiftieth birthday celebrations. In fact, it was complete bliss to see the icons of Carnatic music, M.S Subbulakshmi, Semmangudi Srinivasa Iyer and D.K. Pattammal, together on that occasion.

THE RECORDING

ALBUM: D.K. Pattammal: A Concert Feast from the Music Academy Archives

ACCOMPANISTS: Thirupparkadal Veeraraghavan (violin), T.K. Murthy (kanjira), Sri Rangachari (mridangam)

RELEASED BY: Saregama (2002)

This recording reveals the tradition of rendering a vast repertoire which includes different musical forms like varnam, kritis of different composers of the south, tirippugazh, padams, kavadi chindu and mangalam as a concluding piece. The early twentieth century was a golden era for Carnatic music. A live concert which included all these forms usually took a minimum of three hours of which one hour was sometimes devoted solely to the rendering of ragam-tanam-pallavi. This is a two-disc edition that explores a wide range of Carnatic forms and is a beautiful representative of the south Indian musical tradition.

DISC ONE

1. Swami Ninne (varnam)

Raga: Pantuvarali

Tala: Adi

Composer: Patnam Subramania Iyer

Pantuvarali, also known as Kamavardhini, is a very popular raga in the south. It resembles Raga Purvi Dhanashree of Hindustani music.

2. Janaki Ramana

Raga: Suddha Seemanthini

Tala: Adi

Composer: Thyagaraja

Not many compositions have been composed in this raga. Janaki Ramana is the only composition in this raga by

Thyagaraja. One does not find any compositions by either Dikshitar or Shyama Shastri.

3. Nithamoru

Raga: Kharaharapriya
Tala: Adi
Composer: Ambujam Krishna

Kharaharapriya is a mela raga, closely allied to Hindustani Kafi thaat. Because of its symmetrical tetrachords it is easier to render than its cousin, the Carnatic Bhairavi. Thyagaraja composed innumerable compositions in this raga. This raga is also called Haripriya, delightful to Shiva.

4. Iththarani Meethu (thiruppugazh)

Raga: Asaveri
Composer: Arunagirinathar

Thiruppugazh are sacred hymns in Tamil which are still very popular in Tamil Nadu not only because of their lyrical and spiritual content but also because they give us very valuable information about the lakshyas of different talas, both rare and known.

5. Ranganayakam

Raga: Nayaki
Tala: Adi
Composer: Muthuswami Dikshitar

Nayaki is a scholarly raga of the south which is rendered in slow or vilamba laya with meends or dirgha kampitam of Ga and Ni. Interestingly, if rendered in fast tempo, this changes to another raga named Durbar which has the same aroh-avaroh.

6. Ragam-Tanam-Pallavi (kadaikann)

Raga: Dhanyasi
Tala: Rupakam (Misranadai)

The calibre of a Carnatic musician lies in his command over

improvisation in both raga as well as tala, which is best seen in the RTP exposition. Pattammal was known for her great technical expertise in the rendering of RTP. She would render pallavis set to extremely complicated talas with great aplomb. This recording has a pallavi set to rupakam which is in an intricate misra nadai i.e. the tala has a total of six beats, each beat having seven aksharas.

DISC TWO

1. Kailasapathey

Raga: Kalyani
Tala: Adi
Composer: Mysore Vasudevachar

Raga Kalyani is a very important and popular Carnatic raga. Being an old raga, innumerable compositions can be found in the realms of classical, devotional as well as folk music. This is a mela raga which corresponds to Yaman thaat of Hindustani music. Mysore Vasudevachar, who was both a fine vocalist and a composer, composed kritis which are well-laden with beautiful raga sancharas.

2. Vinaradha Na Manavi

Raga: Chakravaham
Tala: Khandachapu
Composer: Thirupati Narayanaswami

Chakravakom is a melaraga which corresponds to the Ahir Bhairav raga of Hindustani music. 'Vinaradha Na Manavi' in Chakravakom is a rarely heard composition and Pattammal beautifully draws out the essence of the raga through her performance.

3. Vaarijamukhi (Padam)

Raga: Sankarabharanam
Tala: Misrachapu

A Carnatic music concert is divided into two parts. The first part includes both kalpita (pre-composed) sangeeta like the varnam and kritis, and manodharma like the RTP, alapana, niraval and kalpana svaras. The second part, also known as the post-pallavi, includes one or two padams by different composers, some simple devotional and popular folk songs, and often concludes with a tillana which is seen as a befitting finale to the concert. Padams, even though they are rendered post-pallavi, are very scholarly compositions and it requires a highly skilled musician to articulate them correctly. Set to a slow tempo, every nuance of the raga is clearly heard and the artiste has to have a complete command over his/her instrument/voice as well as the raga itself.

4. Rama Rama

Raga: Bhairavi
Tala: Adi
Composer: Kshetragner

Kshetragner (also Kshetrajna) was a contemporary of Venkatamakhi, who evolved the melakarta scheme. His scholarship in composing apoorva ragas and the depth in both melody and sahitya are unparallelled, and this has given him the distinction of being called the father of padams.

5. Kavadi Chindhu

Composer: Annamalai Reddiyar

Kavadi chindus are compositions in praise of Lord Muruga or Kartikeya, the son of Shiva and brother of Ganesha. These songs are sung by devotees who go on a pilgrimage to the shrine of Lord Muruga in Pazhani. The music is simple, brightened with a touch of folk.

6. Mangalam

Composer: Traditional

Every concert ends with a mangalam, a prayer for good omen. Thyagaraja's 'Bhava manasa' in Raga Sourashtram is the most commonly sung mangalam.

CHAPTER 13

Pandit D.V. Paluskar

1921 - 1955

One of the most loved vocalists of his time, Pandit D.V. Paluskar's premature death at the age of 34 was a major loss to the world of Indian classical music. The son and disciple of the legendary Pandit Vishnu Digambar Paluskar, he also trained under Vinayak Rao Patwardhan and Narayan Rao Vyas. He made a great impact in his short career, and even today he has many fans and admirers, with his bhajans being household favourites.

D.V. Paluskar had a wonderfully rich and melodious voice, and his imaginative and complex patterns displayed great workmanship. He became a top ranking artiste in his lifetime and evoked a style of his own that was unique.

THE RECORDING

ALBUM: Golden Milestones

RE-RELEASED BY: Saregama (2003)

1. Raga Lalat (1954): 'Are Man Ram Naam'

The traditional and beautiful Raga Lalit (spelt here as Lalat) in the genius interpretation of D.V. Paluskar is a listener's delight. The omission of Pa and the aesthetic use of a flat re and both madhyams make this track a winner all the way.

2. Raga Bibhas (1950): 'Kaisku Marwa'

A very haunting pentatonic morning raga in which the 4th and 7th notes are absent, this track has an everlasting impact on the listener and records some breathtaking work by Paluskar. The mood is extremely devotional.

3. Raga Bilaskhani Todi (1959): 'Nike Ghunghariya'

Bilaskhani Todi was created by the son and disciple of the great Mian Tansen, Bilas Khan. Legend has it that after Tansen's death, when Bilas Khan sang his creation in honour of his father, the flowers on the maestro's tomb fluttered towards him in the breeze. A raga that has immense sorrow and pathos, D.V. Paluskar's rendition of Bilaskhani Todi moves the listener to tears.

4. Raga Asawari (1948): 'Barhaiya Lao Lao Re'

Now a rare raga, its presentation by this stalwart is unsurpassed.

5. Raga Gaud Sarang (1951): 'Piyu Palan Lagi Mori Ankhiya'

A very popular composition is sung here, often played by instrumentalists as well. Gaud Sarang is one of the most beautiful afternoon ragas. The movement is close to many nearby ragas like Hameer, Anandi and Kedar.

6. Bhajan (1962): 'Payo Ji Maine Raamratan'
This is a timeless and legendary track that continues to have an impact even today.The embellishments to the bhajan by the artiste are ecstatic and full of feeling.

7. Bhajan (1962): 'Thumak Chalat Raamchandra'
Yet another timeless bhajan that was popularized by D.V. Paluskar; a track that surpassed its own time!

8. Raga Hameer (1954): 'Surja Rahi Ho'
One of the most popular ragas amongst vocalists, Hameer has quite a complex movement and is dangerously close to many neighbouring ragas. It has the usage of both the madhyam notes.

9. Raga Tilak Kamod (1959): 'Koelia Bole'
One of the most romantic ragas in the classical music world, Tilak Kamod has an absent 6th note (dha) in its ascent.

10. Raga Kedar (1959): 'Jare Kanre'
In a composition set to jhaptaal, a ten beat time cycle, D.V. Paluskar presents the most mesmerizing Kedar. The use of both the 4th notes (Ma) is extremely intimidating in this raga and in ascent the 2nd and 3rd notes are omitted.

11. Raga Miyan Ki Malhar (1948): 'Aaj Samdhan'
One ofTansen's masterpieces, the name Miyan stands for Mian Tansen. Legend has it that when he sang this raga, it would rain.This raga has the most intriguing usage of both forms of the 7th note.

12. Raga Malkauns (1951): 'Nand Ke Chhaila Dhit'
All the tracks above are effortless masterpieces by Paluskar based on very traditional ragas. He clearly had a magical touch and approach towards them. Malkauns is a pentatonic raga that

omits Re and Pa and it is also an immensely popular raga. There are times when audiences applaud as soon as the name of the raga is announced!

13. Bhajan (1962): 'Jab Janakinath'

The bhajan is based on Raga Khamaj with the madhyam as the prominent note (also called Manjh Khamaj by instrumentalists).

14. Bhajan (1959): 'Chalo Man Ganga Jamuna Teer'

15. Bhajan (1959): 'Raghupati Raghav Raja Ram'

The last two tracks are a fitting finale to a glorious chapter of Indian classical music. The last bhajan has a chorus joining in, as Paluskarji works up a beautiful climax based on Raga Ghara.

CHAPTER 14

Ustad Enayat Khan

1895 – 1938

The genius father and guru of a genius son, Ustad Enayat Khan was one of India's most prominent sitar and surbahar players in the twentieth century. His father was the legendary Ustad Imdad Khan, who taught him the sitar and surbahar. Their school of playing came to be known as the Itawah gharana as that was the city the family belonged to. He married Basiran Begum, the daughter of khayal singer Bande Hassan Khan, and did pioneering work on the sitar.

Ustad Enayat Khan was a contemporary of Ustad Haafiz Ali Khan. Our father would tell us that our grandfather used to find it difficult to perform after Enayat Khan at festivals as he was such a dynamic musician and wonderful performer. Our grandfather would apparently say that every time Enayat Khan performed, the angels would descend.

At a time when music festivals were just gaining popularity at public gatherings in India, as opposed to the earlier trend of intimate gatherings in courts and private homes, Enayat Khan became the ambassador of the sitar and made it reach a wider audience by making it accessible.

Enayat Khan sahib passed away at very young age. Both his sons, Ustad Vilayat Khan and Ustad Imrat Khan, have carried forward his legendary lineage.

THE RECORDING

ALBUM: Great Gharanas
RAGAS: Jogia, Bhairavi, Piloo, Purvi, Khamaj, Bageshwari and Bihari
ACCOMPANIST: Unknown (tabla)
RELEASED BY: Saregama

1. Raga Jogia (Played on sitar): Khan sahib does a very brief alaap for the first few moments and then takes on a fast composition set to teentaal. The opening track speaks for itself about his historic touch to the sitar.

2. Raga Bhairavi (Played on sitar): Khan sahib performs an ornamental alaap in Bhairavi and then plays a drut composition in teentaal. Ironically, we heard his son Ustad Vilayat Khan play the same composition at Carnegie Hall, New York, in 1997. The right-hand master moves that one hears are any instrumentalist's envy.

3. Raga Piloo (Played on sitar): Khan sahib plays a fast composition set to sixteen beats. The colour and flavour of Piloo is explored to the highest levels in this track by this magicial artiste. The piece ends with a beautiful tihai.

4. Raga Purvi (Played on surbahar): The fabulous Purvi, one of the most beautiful Sindhi Prakash ragas, is presented with an alaap of utmost gravity and stature. Khan sahib ends the piece by declaring his name: 'Enayat Khan of Gauripur'.

5. Raga Khamaj (Played on sursaptak): Ustad Enayat Khan had a strong rivalry with a sarod player of his time called Sakhawat Khan. This track was his take on the sarod player where he played an instrument called the sursaptak and said 'Enayat Khan, Sakhawat ka baap' (Enayat Khan, Sakhawat's father) at the end of the recording (it has been edited here). Apparently, Sakhawat Khan had filed a defamation case against Khan sahib, so he renamed one of his sons Sakhawat for a while. The track itself is a landmark track, where one really feels that one is hearing the sarod. Only a genius like Ustad Enayat Khan sahib could do this. The structure and character of Khamaj is at its peak here.

6. Raga Bageshwari (Played on surbahar): Khan sahib plays an alaap in the age-old Raga Bageshwari with the utmost beauty and passion. A truly divine piece!

7. Raga Bihari (Played on sitar): This raga is very close to Raga Tilak Kamod but it has the occasional use of the komal Ni. This was the first ever Bihari to be recorded. In the years to come, it was recorded by a few other instrumentalists, including Ustad Bismillah Khan in the forties and Ustad Amjad Ali Khan in the early seventies. But Enayat Khan sahib takes it to a whole different level.

CHAPTER 15

Ustad Faiyaz Khan

1886 - 1950

A doyen of the Agra school, Ustad Faiyaz Khan's singing has had an immense impact on vocalists even till today. His unique style was created by a blend of subtlety and power, whether he was singing dhrupad, khayal, thumri or ghazal, all of which were simply mind blowing. His voice had a variety of stylizations and many great singers of today get their inspiration from him. His appearance was imposing and he sported a regal moustache. Most of his photographs show him wearing a sherwani, displaying all his medals proudly on his chest, as was the custom in his time.

Khan sahib was born in 1880 into a musically charged family. He

seated at centre: Ustad Haafiz Ali Khan, Ustad Faiyaz Khan and Ustad Ahmed Jaan Thirakhwa

is said to have lost his parents at a very young age and was raised by his illustrious grandfather, Ustad Ghulam Abbas Khan. He received his early training from his grandfather, later moving on to the tutelage of his uncle, Kallan Khan. By the time he was 20, he was a legend, and in 1911 he received the title Aftab-e-Mausiqi from the Maharaja of Mysore.

Even today, vocalists imitate his voice and his pattern of singing. He had a unique way of blending dhrupad and khayal, and gave vocal music a completely new expression. Khan sahib's innovation, layakari and the manner in which he would present each raga was charming all the way.

THE RECORDING

ARTISTE: Ustad Faiyaz Khan
RAGAS: Lalit, Todi, Jaunpuri, Bhairavi, Purvi, Paraj, Puriya, Chhaya Nat, Nat Behag, Sughrai, Darbari, Khamaj, Jaijaiwanti and Kafi
RE-RELEASED BY: Hindusthan Records (1994)

Ustad Faiyaz Khan sahib gave immense importance to the methodical exposition of a composition. Bold, robust voice production became a trend with Khan sahib's imagination and ideology to this school of music. A monumental icon par excellence, be it khayal, dhrupad or thumri, he was a winner in all. This magnificent recording has the timeless 'Jhan Jhan Jhan' in Nat Behag and 'Pavan Chalat' in Chhaya Nat that were household favourites rendered by the maestro.

1. **Raga Lalit** (1940): 'Tarpat Hun'
2. **Raga Todi** (1935): 'Garwa Main'
3. **Raga Jaunpuri** (1940): 'Phool Banki'
4. **Raga Bhairavi Dadra** (1936): 'Chalo Kahe'
5. **Raga Purvi** (1948): 'Madhur Na'
6. **Raga Paraj** (1935): 'Manmohan Brij'
7. **Raga Puriya** (1935): 'Main Kar Aavi'
8. **Raga Chhaya Nat** (1948): 'Pavan Chalat'
9. **Raga Nat Behag** (1936): 'Jhan Jhan Jhan'
10. **Raga Sughrai** (1944): 'Nayna Se'
11. **Raga Darbari** (1945): 'Khayal'
12. **Khamaj Dadra** (1944): 'More Jabanoa'
13. **Raga Jaijaiwanti** (1935): 'More Mandire'
14. **Raga Kafi** (1940): 'Vande Nanakumar'

CHAPTER 16

Dr Gangubai Hangal

1913 - 2009

Gangubai Hangal always believed in the gradual development and unfolding of the raga even though her compositions were short. The phrases and embellishments in her songs are fragile and almost pregnant in that they make the listener wait eagerly for the next phrase.

Dr Gangubai Hangal was born in Hubli, in the former princely state of Mysore. Her mother was a renowned vocalist who sang in the Carnatic style and was her first teacher. In later years, Gangubai trained under the guidance of Sawai Gandharva, who was a direct disciple of

Ustad Abdul Karim Khan of the Kirana gharana. Pandit Bhimsen Joshi was also taught by the same guru.

We had the honour of meeting Gangubai Hangalji only once, in Pune in 1991. She was performing at the Sawai Gandharva Music Festival, just before our father's performance. Since we were playing the tanpura, we met her as she got off the stage after her concert (the stage here is very high, as one needs to make it visible to several thousand people). This was around 2 a.m. It was a time when night-long concerts were still allowed in open-air venues.

Singing for over eight decades, she had a wonderful journey in the world of music and reached a level of sublime divinity. She made no compromises with the purity of her work and became one of the greatest names in the Kirana school of singing. It is indeed sad that we continue to write this chapter a day after she died in Hubli at the age of 97 on July 21, 2009.

THE RECORDING

ALBUM: Golden Milestones
RE-RELEASED BY: Saregama (2003)

Gangubai Hangalji's music was drenched in altruistic devotion. Her melodious movements are sated with pure notes, extensive glissandos and a unique boldness. Intense and pensive, her music inspired true devotion.

Revel in this rich collection of the maestro's favourite ragas, delivered in her robust and uninhibited voice. Interestingly, track 12 is Gangubaiji's own interpretation of Raga Bageshwari, where one hears a sharp 3rd and a sharp 7th note (Ga and Ni) along with the flat ones. A liberty that only geniuses can take!

1. **Raga Miyan Malhar** (1935): 'Kahe Ladli Lad Ladai'

2. **Raga Bhairav:** 'Ey Banata Banaay'

3. **Raga Jogia** (1935): 'Hari Ka Bhed Na Payo'

4. **Raga Hindol** (1931): 'Laal Jinkar Ho'

5. **Raga Marwa** (1950): 'Sun Sun Batiyan'

6. **Raga Puriya** (1934): 'Rangkar Rasia Aaye'

7. **Raga Bhupali:** 'Nandiya Jaage'

8. **Raga Kamod Tarana** (1934): 'Tana Dere Na'

9. **Raga Deskar** (1931): 'Amita Mat Mashi Balaji'

10. **Raga Durga** (1935): 'Darshan Bin Ankhiyan'

11. **Raga Khambavati** (1935): 'Hari Khelat Brij Main Holi'

12. **Raga Bageshwari** (1933): 'Chan More Saiyyan Balam'

13. **Raga Malkauns** (1933): 'Mero Mann Har Lino Shamsunder'

14. **Raga Bahar:** 'Saundhe Sugandh'

15. **Raga Chandrakauns** (1980): 'Kab Ghar Aayo'

CHAPTER 17

Ustad Ghulam Mustafa Khan

1931 –

One of India's foremost singers, Ustad Ghulam Mustafa Khan sahib today is an institution by himself. A representative of the Sahaswan Rampur gharana, he is an icon for vocalists and is a living example of a monumental figure in the world of Indian classical music. He continues to train many disciples and has taught a diverse range of artistes including composer A.R. Rahman, playback singers Sonu Nigan and Shaan and ghazal superstar Hariharan. Ghulam Mustafa Khan is the grandson of Ustad Inayat Hussain Khan of the Sahaswan gharana, who was the son-in-law of Ustad Haddu Khan sahib, the pioneer of the Gwalior gharana.

Khan sahib was born on March 3, 1931, in Badaun, Uttar Pradesh, into a family of great musicians. He was initiated into music by his father Ustad Waris Hussain Khan and later learnt from Ustad Fida Hussain Khan, the father of the famous maestro Ustad Nissar Hussain Khan. Later, Ustad Nissar Hussain Khan took him under his tutelage.

We met Khan sahib for the first time in Mumbai in 1999. Khan sahib had invited our father for dinner at his Mumbai residence and Ayaan had accompanied him for that memorable dinner. The two artistes sang songs and discussed music, and the evening was a special and inspiring one. After this, we met Khan sahib when he came to New Delhi to receive the Haafiz Ali Khan Award in 2000 where he also sang after the award ceremony.

Both of us will always be indebted to Khan sahib as he very graciously agreed to sing for us while we were composing the score of a film called *American Daylight* in Mumbai in 2004. The film was directed by Oscar-winner Roger Christian and was produced by Bobby Bedi of Kaleidoscope Entertainment. Although the film never saw the 'daylight' of a release, the music, luckily, was released by Sony. Khan sahib sang the most extraordinary Raga Darbari in Track 15 which created magic on screen. We were in no position to offer anything to a man of his stature but the love and affection he bestowed upon us is something we will never forget. We recall that Ustad Vilayat Khan sahib had passed away a few days before the recording took place and as we spoke of Ustad Vilayat Khan in the studio after the recording, Khan sahib broke down. It pained him no end to see the greats from the world of Indian classical music leaving one after another.

We also met Ustad Ghulam Mustafa Khan at his 75th birthday celebrations at Nehru Centre in Mumbai where a three-day music festival took place and our father concluded the festival. Khan sahib is an artiste far ahead of his time and has been a trendsetter for many vocalists around him who still keep a close watch on what he will do next.

THE RECORDING

ALBUM: Ustad Ghulam Mustafa Khan
RAGAS: Saraswati and Nayaki Kanhara
ACCOMPANISTS: Unknown
RELEASED BY: Saregama

1. Raga Saraswati

'More Man Bhaye', khayal in vilambit ektaal
'Sajan Aaye', khayal in drut teentaal

ASCENDING: Sa Re ma Pa Dha ni
DESCENDING: Sa ni Dha Pa ma Re

Although this raga is called Saraswati, it is hardly played any more. It is one of the most beautiful and haunting ragas from the world of classical music. The track begins with the most sublime development of the raga. Some great lower octave movements are heard. Honestly, not many artistes, particularly instrumentalists, would go in the direction of even wanting to present this raga just because of its musical challenge. The typical phrase 'Re ma Pa Dha ni' resounds as the raga gradually unfolds in a slow composition set to a 12-beat time cycle. Intricate firework gamaks are heard and some breathtaking complex sargams are explored in this composition. The drut khayal, the fast composition, flows effortlessly. One hears some divine taans and electrifying musicianship through this piece.

2. Raga Nayaki Kanhara

'Mag Waran Varoon Pinarwa', khayal vilambit ektaal
'Saghar Banra', khayal in drut teentaal

This is one of the most beautiful ragas from the Kanhara family, more commonly presented by vocalists. Khan sahib sings this raga in its purest form and captivates the listener from start to finish. Once again, the wondrous gamaks and taans are heard in the most technically complex manner, going up all three octaves. Khan sahib is at his creative best in this recording and his work speaks volumes for itself. The khayal composition in teentaal carries a timeless old-world charm.

CHAPTER 18

Girija Devi

1929 -

One of India's greatest singing queens, Girija Devi is in a league of her own. Born in the holy city of Benaras in 1929, she was shown the oceanic world of music by her gurus Sarjuprasad Misra and Shrichand Mishra. She first learnt the khayal style and later the captivating thumri style. She is truly a chip of the old block and perhaps one of the only remaining artistes of an era that was the pinnacle of creativity and the domain of disciplined practice.

Her approach and her essence are unique. She creates magic and an uncanny flavour whether she presents a khayal or the lighter elements of Indian classical music like kajri, hori and jhoola.

Our first interaction with Girija Bua was in 1995 for a very personal family celebration. It was our mother's 50th birthday and Girija Deviji was singing. It was a surprise, so she was also a part of the surprise. She sang so emotionally that day! She said that she didn't perform at private gatherings but because of the love and relationship she shared with our father and the regard she had for our family heritage, she said that she had no choice but to come and sing. The following morning she also visited our home.

We clearly remember her wonderful recital at the Dover Lane Music Festival in Kolkata before our father took centrestage. When we played in Varanasi in the winter of 2000 for Rajan Sajan Mishra's father's (Pandit Hanuman Prasad Mishra) first death anniversary, she was present in the concert hall at Nagri Natak Mandali. The next day she invited us for breakfast in her residence. After this, we had to go for breakfast to Pandit Kishan Maharaj's house. So that morning, we had two breakfasts! This was all an extension of the love and respect that these great artistes had for our father and his ancestors. We truly feel humbled and fortunate to have had the hands of these legends on our heads.

In 2005, our father was to perform with Girija Devi at Opera De Munt in Belgium, which is a festival only for vocalists. They even recorded an album together called *Confluence: Meeting of Minds and*

Melodies released by Navras Records that year. Unfortunately, she was unable to be a part of that concert as she had fallen sick at that time. Today she retains her supreme status and is one of the most loved and respected 'devi's of Indian classical music.

THE RECORDING

ALBUM: Song of the Seasons, Girija Devi
TRACKS: Kaisi Dhoom Machai (Hori Kafi), Raat Ham Dekhelee Sapanwa Ho Rama (Chaiti), Kahanwa Mano Ho Radha Rani (Kajri), Jhoola Dhirey Se Jhulau Banwari (Jhoola)
ACCOMPANISTS: Pandit Kishan Maharaj (tabla), Ramesh Mishra (sarangi)
RELEASED BY: Music Today (1993)

Seasonal ragas have always been an integral subject in the world of Indian classical music. Spring, monsoon and many other factors associated with nature have very strong representations in the raga world. We cannot confine the genre of kajri, hori, jhoola, etc. as just a classical piece or a folk piece. Rather, it's a confluence of both with the element of spontaneity being very prominent. The text is usually Brajbhasha, Avadhi, Khari Boli, Bojpuri and other such dialects that are basically a merger of classical and folk. This form of music is, as we said, very individualistic in order to accommodate moods and emotions. Some of these tracks are sung on specific months of the year; for instance during the Holi festival of colour, the hori is sung where the lyrics talk of the mischief of Lord Krishna whereas rainy season songs like kajri, jhoola, etc. are for the month of Sawan.

Each and every track is sung from the heart and gives the true essence of this world of music. What makes this recording all the more special is the tabla accompaniment of the great Pandit Kishan Maharaj. He also comes from Varanasi which makes this album more authentic. He gives celestial support to Girija Devi and plays some of the most iconic laggis at the end of a few tracks. A collector's album and an album that shows its listeners a way back in time.

CHAPTER 19

Ustad Haafiz Ali Khan

1882 - 1972

It is indeed hard to describe the prophet of sarod. Dada Abba, as we would have addressed him, passed away in 1972 in New Delhi. We never got to meet him, but we have grown up hearing about him and feeling his presence in our everyday life. Haafiz Ali Khan sahib was a legend in his time. He was called the godfather of instrumental music by his contemporaries and even by the generation after him. He has inspired all the instrumentalists of his time and also after. He was a simple man and a man of principles. He never cared about the consequences but did as his heart pleased. He was a purist, so much so that he would

do drastic things to maintain his principles like asking the President of India to save the purity of a raga!

The tradition of the Senia gharana of Ustad Pyar Khan and Ustad Jafar Khan, direct descendants of the line of Tansen, was Ustad Haafiz Ali Khan's rich inheritance. As his father Ustad Nanneh Khan died when he was still young, he was on a personal mission to learn his art. He enhanced his knowledge in dhrupad and dhamar under the guidance of Pandits Chukkhalalji and Ganeshilalji Chaube of Brindavan, descendants of Swami Haridas, Mian Tansen's guru. Finally, to quench his thirst for knowledge, he sat at the feet of Ustad Wazir Khan of Rampur. By accepting Ustad Haafiz Ali Khan as his disciple, Ustad Wazir Khan broke the convention of teaching only family members. The man himself symbolised originality and purity. Awards came in profusion throughout his life.

Dada Abba never believed in recording his performances as he felt that the music would be played in social gatherings and in situations where music would be heard with less respect and therefore humiliated. Hence, the recordings that are available from this sarod maestro are only those that were released from his radio broadcasts in the later stage of his life. It has indeed been a great loss to the world of music not to have the music of this icon recorded during his younger days.

THE RECORDING

ALBUM: Sangeet Sadhak Ustad Haafiz Ali Khan
RAGAS: Mian Ki Malhar, Sanjha Tarini, Bhairavi and Chandra Bhankar
ACCOMPANIST: Unknown
RELEASED BY: Saregama in collaboration with All India Radio (2005)

1. Raga Mian Ki Malhar: Every stroke of Haafiz Ali Khan sahib was rapid fire. The alaap explores the usage of both the Nishads in the most poetic manner. Mian Ki Malhar has the uniqueness of using both nishads in very close quarters. A raga created by the great Mian Tansen, it is today one of the most popular rainy season ragas.

Haafiz Ali Khan never liked to prolong a raga beyond half an hour as he felt that it was all repetition, which is indeed true. The composition has a deep impact and places the ragas in very little time. The legendary Haafiz Ali Khan ekehra taans, inspired by vocalists, are played effortlessly in this recording. In instrumental music, certain taans are almost impossible to produce as an instrument cannot do that which a human voice can. However, Haafiz Ali Khan successfully produced these vocal ekehra taans with his plectrum on the sarod.

While the cycle of sixteen beats is on, some alaap patterns are also played and also some jhala movements played with a lot of elaboration. Khan sahib used to tune his sarod in a special manner where it was not just the tonic that one could hear in the chikari but also the Ni. The true tonic is an interesting point. It depends on what one means by tonic. One way is to say that Sa is the tonic and leave it at that. Western ears may mistake the F (Ma) for the tonic, which would perhaps create a greater sense of harmony, a feature that is important in Western classical music.

2. Raga Sanjha Tarini: This raga is a creation of Ustad Haafiz Ali Khan sahib. Inspired by Purvi and Lalita Gauri, this raga has the usage of the shuddha Dha (6th) along with the komal dha. The beauty is that this raga sounds just like a traditional raga made at the time of its inspiration. Dada Abba uses a thick string as the fifth main string on his sarod, and he is the first artiste to have done so. When one hears this raga, it feels as if this was created at the same time as Purvi and Lalita Gauri as a third entity. In time, other instrumentalists started using this string, both in the sarod as well as the sitar. The flavour and colour of this evening raga are completely meditative and blissful. The composition is set to sixteen beats.

3. Raga Bhairavi: The album concludes with Raga Bhairavi. Typically vocal phrases of Bhairavi are heard in the brief alaap. The play with the volume of the plectrum by Haafiz Ali Khan sahib only makes his music sound like a song, as though the music comes from a human voice, not a sarod. Some of the most unpredictable and breathless combinations of notes are used here. Bhairavi gives the freedom to use all twelve notes of music, though the usage has to be aesthetic. The composition is in a fast tempo set to sixteen beats.

4. Chandra Bhankar: This raga was also Ustad Haafiz Ali Khan's creation. From the alaap itself, one can sense the uniqueness of the great man who was unquestionably far ahead of his time in his imagination and principles. Interestingly, the pace of the alaap is somewhat faster than usual, almost giving it an element of jor in many moments. This raga has flashes of Jogia and Ramkali garlanded together. The composition is set to teentaal. On starting the composition, Haafiz Ali Khan sahib does some vocal-like improvisation at a slower pace, that sound almost like short alaap patterns. Soon after, the ekehra taans are heard.

The slow alaap-oriented patterns are repeated quite a few times in different areas in both lower and upper octaves. This raga has both the 4th notes (Ma) in flat and sharp and a flat 2nd (re) and 6th (dha). The use of some ecstatic combinations of notes testifies as to who he was. The track ends with a combination of a jhala (crescendo) and honeyed vocal-like elements with the sum of the composition played again.

CHAPTER 20

Pandit Hari Prasad Chaurasia

1938 –

It is very rare to go into a record shop and not see a recording of Pandit Hari Prasad Chaurasia, the master of the bansuri or bamboo flute. One of India's most popular artistes, he is a man on a mission and defies his age to meet his commitments. He is in Mumbai today, Paris tomorrow and San Francisco the day after, with performances on all three days. His endearing persona and ease with people of all ages enhance his popularity.

We first met Hari uncle at the same time as we met Pandit Shiv Kumar Sharma during the ITC Sangeet Sammelan in 1989. But our interaction with his family started when he made a thirteen-episode

At home, with Hari uncle and our father

television series called *Sadhana* in 1988, featuring contemporary Indian artistes. The programme went on to become a huge hit. After that, we have met Hari uncle on numerous occasions over the years, and he has always offered us generous guidance and advice.

Hari Prasad Chaurasia began his musical training by learning vocal with Pandit Raja Ram of Benaras. A flute recital by Pandit Bholanath left a deep impact on him, thus starting his historic love affair with the instrument. At the young age of 19, he got a job with All India Radio in Cuttack and was transferred to Mumbai after five years. Here, he became a disciple of Annapurna Devi, the daughter of Ustad Allauddin Khan of Maihar, and consolidated his musical skill.

Hari uncle's words of encouragement and warmth upon our first electronic venture *Reincarnation*, which released in 2005, left a deep impression on us. Earlier in 2002, we shared a very memorable evening in Edinburgh with him and our father during the music festival there. We also recall attending his musical evening featuring many famous performers, at Shivaji Park, Mumbai, in 1991, to raise funds for his institution. A master of his craft, he is an exemplar to the music world.

THE RECORDING

ALBUM: Indian Night Live Stuttgart '88

RAGA: Malkauns

ACCOMPANISTS: Zakir Hussain (tabla), Sweta Jhaveri and Durga Jasraj (tanpura)

RELEASED BY: Chhanda Dhara (1989)

One of the most beautiful and appealing pentatonic night ragas, Malkauns is heard at its best in this recording. The composition is in rupaktaal, which is based on a seven-beat time cycle (3 + 2 + 2), followed by a drut in teentaal. Hari Prasad Chaurasia makes his flute sing like a human voice. The alaap is played from the soul and one feels as though time has stood still. The alaap is followed by the jor and jhala. It is amazing to see how these sequences are established in a wind instrument that has no chikari (drone strings). Ustad Zakir Hussain uses his magical hands to the fullest, as always.

CHAPTER 21

Ustad Imdad Khan

1848 – 1920

The founder of the Etawah gharana of sitar playing, Ustad Imdad Khan was one of the greatest sitar and surbahar players of his time. He was a pioneering artiste who performed widely all over the Indian subcontinent and it is said that he even played for Queen Victoria during her visit to India.

Imdad Khan sahib learnt from his father Sahabdad Khan, a trained vocalist and sitar player. As Imdad Khan's musical journey progressed, he developed a technique and style that were very unique. Imdad Khan was also trained by the legendary beenkar Bande Ali Khan, a disciple and son-in-law of Ustad Haddu Khan (of the brothers Haddu-Hassu Khan).

He had two sons who became central figures in the world of Indian instrumental music, Ustad Enayet Khan and Ustad Wahid Khan.

The most famous story we have heard of Ustad Imdad Khan was that he was a fanatic as far as practising was concerned, to the point that when he travelled by train he would get off at the next station when it was time for him to practise. We also heard from our father and Ustad Vilayat Khan that since they did not have watches back then, they timed the level of an artiste's practice with large, thick candles. An artiste would play until the candle burned out. So they would say that Ustad Imdad Khan is 'a four candle practised artiste'!

THE RECORDING

ALBUM: Great Gharanas

RAGAS: Bhairav, Jaunpuri Todi, Jaunpuri, Kafi, Khamaj, Yaman, Behag, Sohini and Darbari Kanhara

ACCOMPANIST: Unknown (tabla)

RECORDED IN: 1905 and 1910

RELEASED BY: Saregama

This recording consists of only three-minute ragas from this monumental artiste. In those days, artistes would say their name out loud after each piece, and in this compilation of three-minute records, you can hear the artiste say Imdad Khan after one of the pieces.

1. Raga Bhairav: Khan sahib plays a very fast composition full of vigour and virtuosity. The tantra kaari ang (an instrumental syllable style) are played at an unimaginable speed.

2. Raga Jaunpuri Todi: Khan sahib plays an alaap for all three minutes of this raga. But the entire character of the raga is captured within those few minutes. One can hear the usage of the kharajh string that was not used by later generations of his family.

3. Raga Jaunpuri: The track starts with a jor and jhala at a high speed and it remains constant and the beauty of Raga Jaunpuri is effortlessly heard.

4. Raga Kafi: Khan sahib plays a beautiful Kafi with breathtaking right-hand work that shows his wondrous command over the sitar. The track ends with an equally fabulous jhala. The timeless colours of Kafi, typically vocal in flavour, cannot go unnoticed.

5. Raga Khamaj: A raga that is inseparable from the Imdad Khan family today, Khan sahib plays one of the most beautiful compositions of Raga Khamaj. The tantrakaari element shines limitlessly here along with some lightning taans.

6. Raga Yaman: A drut composition is played in teentaal. In fact, all the compositions in these tracks are played in sixteen beats. Some very interesting patterns are played with timeless work that goes down history.

7. Raga Behag: A breathtaking composition is played and yet again, played at its very best. Indeed, this is a surreal track that shows Imdad Khan sahib's genius in no time.

8. Raga Sohini: This is usually a very rare raga for instrumentalists. However, this track of Sohini by Khan sahib rubbishes this statement. His composition sounds as though it was made just for the sitar.

9. Raga Darbari Kanhara: A fast composition is played set to teentaal.This work is in every way what we call a master's recording.

CHAPTER 22

Pandit Jasraj

1930 –

Veteran vocalist Pandit Jasraj belongs to the Mewati gharana of Rajasthan. He is one of the most sought after singers at musical conferences and soirees, and has made a major contribution in popularizing Indian classical vocal all over the world, especially among the younger generation. His amazing voice moves effortlessly over three octaves and his music has a sublime quality that touches the listener deeply.

Pandit Jasraj lost his father, Pandit Motiram, when he was just three years old and received his musical training largely under his elder brother, Pandit Maniram. He was also deeply moulded by his spiritual

mentor Maharaja Jaywant Singhji Waghela, a musical scholar himself. Today, Pandit Jasraj is a household name for music lovers, to whom he has endeared himself through his practical mastery and creativity.

We first met Pandit Jasraj in 1988 at the concert of our father's student Abhik Sarkar at Kamani Auditorium, New Delhi. Pandit Jasraj was scheduled to sing later in the evening. We met him backstage and he pulled our cheeks affectionately. We grew to call him Taayaji and later heard him sing on numerous occasions in Mumbai, New Delhi, New York and New Jersey. Among all our father's contemporaries, he has been one of the most encouraging to us as artistes. He has invited us to perform, jointly and individually, for the annual music festival that he organizes in Hyderabad in memory of his father and his guru — Pandit Motiram Pandit Maniram Sangeet Samaroh.

Pandit Jasraj has schools in his name in various cities in the US, as well as a concert hall named after him at the Hanuman Temple in New Jersey. A recipient of the Padma Vibhushan and the Sangeet Natak Akademi Award among many other accolades, he has encouraged and presented his disciples to the concert stage, and many of them are well-known artistes today.

THE RECORDING

ALBUM: Ornamental Voice of Pandit Jasraj
RAGAS: Nayaki Kanhara, Adana, Bhajan and Bhairavi
ACCOMPANISTS: Zakir Hussain (tabla), Sultan Khan (sarangi), Shefali Nag and Durga Jasraj (tanpura)
RELEASED BY: Chhanda Dhara (1989)

1. Raga Nayaki Kanhara: The album begins with Nayaki, one of the most endearing ragas from the Kanhara family. This family has several night ragas, the most popular ones being Bageshwari Kanhara, Kausi Kanhara, Darbari Kanhara and Abhogi Kanhara. Pandit Jasraj's presentation of Raga Nayaki Kanhara is perfection at its best. From the structure to the improvisation, it is a winner all the way. He is accompanied by sarangi maestro Sultan Khan, who provides excellent support.

2. Raga Adana: Raga Adana is a 'Pandit Jasraj special'. It is sung on demand at most of his concerts. The raga is sung largely in the uttarang, the upper octave. The lyrics here are 'Mata Kali Maa' and the composition is set in teentaal.

3. Raga Bhairavi: This is followed by a signature bhajan of Pandit Jasraj and the recording here is quite sublime. The album ends with a gorgeous Bhairavi in praise of Shri Kameshwar. All the tracks are wonderfully supported by Ustad Zakir Hussain on the tabla.

CHAPTER 23

Surashri Kesarbai Kerkar

1892 - 1977

Surashri Kesarbai Kerkar received her musical training from the legendary Ustad Abdul Karim Khan and also from the vocalist Ramakrishnabua Vaze. After she moved from her home state Goa to Mumbai, she learnt under Ustad Alladiya Khan, the founder of the Jaipur Atrauli gharana.

A diva of her time, Kesarbai Kerkar was a contemporary of our grandfather, Ustad Haafiz Ali Khan. Her voice was sheer magic and her movements over the three octaves were simply effortless. Kesarbai was one of the most sought after artistes of her time. She was awarded the Padma Bhushan in 1969 and also received the title 'Surashri' in 1948.

In those days, an artiste had to prove his or her worth in three minutes on 78 rpm records. The short recordings from the 1930s and 40s that we have highlighted are just a teaser to her genius and greatness. This album can move you to tears just by its approach, imagination and simplicity. The statement that music cannot lie is fully illustrated here.

THE RECORDING

ALBUM: Vintage 78 RPM Recordings Surashri Kesarbai Kerkar
RAGAS: Vibhas, Todi, Sughrai, Chaiti, Multani, Mand, Bhajan, Puriya Dhanashri, Tilak Kamod, Hori Khamaj, Shankara, Jaijaiwanti and Bhairavi
RELEASED BY: Saregama

Kesarbai Kerkar made a probability into a possibility. Just as you don't need to see the entire film to understand an actor's screen presence or acting capabilities, here too, each three-minute track is enough to speak of this doyen's genius, musical skill and imagination. One of the best collections of Kesarbai's for sure!

1. **Raga Vibhas:** 'Mora Re'

2. **Raga Todi:** 'Haan Re Daiya'

3. **Raga Sughrai:** 'Main Ke'

4. **Raga Chaiti:** 'Saiya Bhala Jogi'

5. **Raga Multani:** 'In Durjan'

6. **Raga Mand:** 'Aankh Daalya Gulal'

7. **Bhajan:** 'Mero Kya Bigaega'

8. **Raga Puriya Dhanashri:** 'Atahi Prachand'

9. **Raga Tilak Kamod:** 'Sur Sangat'

10. **Hori Khamaj:** 'Aaye Shyam Mose Khelan Holi'

11. **Raga Shankara:** 'Ayeri More'

12. **Raga Mand:** 'Balam Mora'

13. **Raga Jaijaiwanti:** 'Piya Hum'

14. **Bhairavi Thumri:** 'Kaise Samjhaun'

CHAPTER 24

Pandit Kishan Maharaj

1923 - 2008

Kishan Maharaj, the renowned tabla virtuoso, was born on his namesake's birthday, Shri Krishna Janmashtami, in Benaras, and began his practical training at a very early age under his father, Pandit Hari Maharaj. After his father's death, he trained under his uncle, the famous Pandit Kanthe Maharaj of the Benaras gharana. As a young man on a musical quest, he left home and spent several months at the Sankat Mochan temple in Benaras, still renowned for its annual musical conference, where he practised under a strict regime. He made his debut as a full-fledged performer as early as 1940 at the All Indian Music Conference in Benaras. This was the beginning of a long

and prodigious career spanning prestigious music festivals all over India and accompanying the best artistes in the country. Through his skill and hard work, he added a new dimension of originality to his already famous family's contribution to 'taal-vidya'.

Pandit Kishan Maharaj was one our father's closest colleagues. They shared a special bond for over forty years until his death in 2008. A true star of his instrument, Taayaji was a trendsetter in the world of tabla. All young tabla players wanted to be like him, talk like him, look like him and of course, play like him. However, his ways were unique to himself, and no one else could really pull it off.

Pandit Kishan Maharaj performed at festivals around the world and was awarded the Padmashri and Padma Vibhushan. We were very fortunate to perform with him in New Delhi in 1993 at the Haafiz Ali Khan Memorial Award function. He affectionately announced that he had done a hat trick with our family that day, as he had performed with our grandfather, father, and now with us. His love for our family was beyond just performing with our father. Whenever he was in Delhi, he would call and come home for lunch or dinner, without fail. He and Abba shared an uncanny rapport, and he had a very special affection for both of us. We were with him in his house in Varanasi in 2008 when he had a cerebral stroke, and we rushed him to the hospital. Taayaji did not regain consciousness and passed away a few

days later. His death marks the end of a glorious era in tabla vaadan. There will never be another Kishan Maharaj. A true 'Sangeet Martand'.

THE RECORDING

ALBUM: Pandit Kishan Maharaj - A Live Tabla Solo Recital at Queen Elizabeth Hall, London, July 1995
TRACKS: Tabla solo in Teentaal
ACCOMPANISTS: Ramesh Mishra (sarangi), Jyoti Bhawalkar (tanpura)
RELEASED BY: Navras Records (1996)

This album is a wonderful example of the Benaras school of tabla playing. Pandit Kishan Maharaj appears to be in a most relaxed state of mind and goes into every detail of the subtle nuances of his presentation. He recites every rhythm syllable before playing it on the tabla. Rhythmic variations from the amad to the famous adi chalan, and forms like the Banarasi thekas, qaidas and paltas, are showcased in the most refined and majestic manner. Complementing this are all the traditional elements from the Benaras gharana, making it a true collector's item. Although the recording was done towards the latter part of his life, it captures the impressive journey and the stunning canvas of this virtuoso.

CHAPTER 25

Kishori Amonkar

1931 -

Kishori Amonkar is a true nightingale of India. The significant quality of her music along with her technique and her melancholic tone leave a mesmeric impact on her listeners. Calling her music eclectic or captivating is an understatement. A recipient of the Sangeet Natak Akademi Award and the Padma Bhushan, Kishori Amonkar has also received the title 'Gana Saraswati'.

We first met Kishori Amonkarji in Mumbai in 1994 at the time when her mother, the great Moghubai Kurdikar, was receiving the Haafiz Ali Khan Award at the Nehru Centre. Kishori Aunty was to sing

after the award ceremony. That evening, she sang Raga Chhaya Nat, Rasiya Kanhara and ended with a bhajan.

We had heard many stories about how severe and unpredictable she was but we feel that she has been misunderstood. She has a side that we have closely seen which is full of love and affection. Today, Kishori Amonkar has many disciples who are carrying forward her message and approach. She has always encouraged her disciples to aim for the highest levels and constantly makes them sing with her at the biggest of festivals and venues in India and abroad. In fact, most of her recent albums have a student singing alongside, which is rather unusual for a senior artiste of her era.

We had the opportunity to interact with Kishori Amonkar once more in 1995 when she came to New Delhi to sing for our father's fiftieth birthday. What a concert that was — the Kamani auditorium was packed to the fullest and the two of us had to sit in the aisles! She sang Raga Bhoop followed by Sampoorna Malkauns and finally a bhajan. Shafaat Ahmed Khan accompanied her on the tabla.

Kishori Amonkar received the Haafiz Ali Khan Award in 1998 in Gwalior. Her award was presented by Sonia Gandhi and the other awardee that evening was Pandit Shankar Ghosh. She is truly one of India's greatest singers, and one who has lived her life by her own convictions.

THE RECORDING

ALBUM: Kishori Amonkar Excels
RAGA: Hansdhwani
ACCOMPANISTS: Pradip Dixit (tabla), Purushottam Walawalkar (harmonium), Vidya Bhagwat and Nandini Bedekar (tanpura)
RECORDED BY: Avinash Oak
RELEASED BY: PAN Music (1993)

The album has a fabulous 72 minutes of Raga Hansdhwani. The recording starts with a composition in a slow version of teentaal called Addhaa. The lyrics are 'Ganapanti Vighana Harana', a composition in praise of Lord Ganesha. The raga is disclosed gradually with extensive detail and beauty. This composition follows to the second track with the most imaginative improvisation. This is in fact the most unique part of Indian classical music where we don't read, write or memorize anything. It is an oral tradition carrying on for generations. Within a raga, we improvise within the set rules of ascending and descending notes. The basic mantra is 'freedom within the discipline.' What we are taught first passes to our mind, and thereon to our soul. There are times when you get off stage and realize that what you just performed was with the help of a spiritual medium. You were just a tool! A concert or, for that matter, a recording can never be repeated in just the same way nor can the improvisations.

The following composition, again in teentaal, is in medium tempo. The lyrics here are 'Aaja Sajana Sanga'. The album concludes with a tarana, which is a set of musical syllables without meaning, introduced by Amir Khusru in the thirteenth century.

Kishori Amonkar's signature firework taans go right up to the upper octave and are heard from the medium tempo composition right till the end of the tarana which ends at a higher tempo. Raga Hansdhwani is a very popular raga from the south Indian style of classical music. Today, it is a favourite of both vocalists and instrumentalists. It is a pentatonic raga and the combination of notes is:

ASCENDING: Sa Re Ga Pa Ni
DESCENDING: Sa Ni Pa Ga Re

The 4th note Pa is the predominant note in this raga. Theoretically it is called the vaadi note.

It is indeed rare to have a north Indian vocalist present such an elaborate version of Hansdhwani.

CHAPTER 26

Pandit Kumar Gandharva

1924 - 1992

A man who surpassed his own time, Pandit Kumar Gandharva was a cult figure for his followers. He refused to be tied down by any individual gharana or tradition and took the music world by storm through his personal interpretation. Born on April 8, 1924, as Shivputra Sidharamayya Komkali, he later assumed the name Kumar Gandharva. He showed prodigious talent even at the age of ten when he first sang in public. Not many people are aware that he had only one lung, in spite of which his singing was unmatched.

He is the perfect example of an artiste who sees a raga as a living entity and gives it the same amount of respect that one would give god. He illustrates the thin line between music and spirituality. Kumar Gandharva also sang other genres like devotional songs (bhajans), folk songs, etc. He was a man immersed in experimentation on a large scale, a thinker and a performer who was absorbed in a deep exploration of the innumerable aspects of music.

The celebrated singer, known for his innovative style and fondness for creating new ragas, was honoured with the Padma Bhushan, Padma Vibhushan and the Kalidas Samman. We never got the opportunity to hear Pandit Kumar Gandharva on stage, but we did hear his wife, Vasundhara Komkali, in 1992 in New Delhi, when she sang after collecting the posthumous Haafiz Ali Khan Award for her husband, who had sadly passed away a few months before the ceremony. It was the end of yet another glorious chapter of Indian classical music.

THE RECORDING

ALBUM: Golden Milestones
RAGAS: Bhairavi, Mishra Kafi, Bageshri, Ramkali, Shankara, Adana, Dhani, Gaud Malhar, Deskar, Jaunpuri, Kamod, Kedar Mand
RE-RELEASED BY: Saregama (2004)

Interestingly, in this compilation, the first four tracks were recorded when Kumar Gandharva was a child, and from Track 5 we hear an older voice. The initial tracks make it clear that he was a child prodigy, singing extremely complex patterns effortlessly and that too in ragas that need special care. This recording has an interesting variety of popular compositions, bhajans, and a range of ragas.

1. **Raga Bhairavi:** 'Kaheko Jhuti Bano Batiyan'

2. **Raga Mishra Kafi:** 'Aaj Kaisi Brij Mein'

3. **Raga Bageshri:** 'Gundh Laori Malania'

4. **Raga Ramkali:** 'Sagari Rain Ki Jaagi'

5. **Raga Shankara:** 'Sir Pe Dhari Gang'

6. **Raga Adana:** 'Have Main Ne Tosi'

7. **Bhajan:** 'Jaag Piya Re' Lyrics — Kabir

8. **Bhajan:** 'Sanvali Mhari Aaj' Lyrics — Meerabai

9. **Raga Dhani:** 'Aai Rut Aai'

10. **Raga Gaud Malhar:** 'Na Batati Tu Pahachan'

11. **Raga Deskar:** 'Ja Ja Re Bhanvara Ja'

12. **Raga Jaunpuri:** 'Hari Hari Ja'

13. **Bhajan:** 'Main Janu Nahin' Lyrics — Meerabai

14. **Bhajan:** 'Mhari Preet Nibhajo' Lyrics — Meerabai

15. **Raga Kamod:** 'Mori Nain Lagan Laagi'

16. **Raga Kedar Mand:** 'Lade Bira Mhane Chunari'

CHAPTER 27

Dr L. Subramaniam

1947 -

Dr L. Subramaniam has played the violin in both Carnatic and Western music traditions. His journey has been a unique one and his contribution towards the violin has not been matched by any other Indian. He is a genius India has never seen before, and a unique violinist on the world stage too.

However, this is one artiste whom we didn't know in our childhood, and had not even had the opportunity to meet in the eighties and nineties. The first time that we met Dr Subramaniam was in 2002 in New Delhi, at an event organized by the Sahara Group at Darbar Hall, Taj Palace Hotel. He had recently married Kavita Krishnamurty. Our interaction with him started because of an album that he wanted to record with our father. The recording was done in Bangalore, after which a recital took place that year at the Esplanade in Singapore, where Abba performed and we accompanied him in the first half. It was after these interactions that we kept meeting Dr Subramaniam on different occasions.

L. Subramaniam's technique and approach combine authenticity with modernity. He has done some pathbreaking collaborations and experimentation that will be remembered for a long time by students of music and listeners alike. Interestingly, he is the only artiste who has played duets with both Ali Akbar Khan and Amjad Ali Khan, the two icons of the sarod.

THE RECORDING

ALBUM: L. Subramaniam En Concert
RAGA: Kalyani, Ragamallika
ACCOMPANISTS: V. Kamakalar Rao (mridangam), Viji Subramaniam (tanpura)
RELEASED BY: Radio France (1985)

1. Raga Kalyani: Tala eka (four beat cycle)

Raga Kalyani is number 65 of the 72 parent melakartas. Melakarta is a compilation of the basic ragas in Carnatic music. They are the 72 parent ragas from which other ragas may be formed. In north Indian music, the thaat is the equivalent of melakarta. There are a total of 10 thaats in north Indian music. This is useful for a theoretical knowledge of north Indian classical music but when it comes to performing, there are many elements that are quite questionable and controversial.

The basic framework of Raga Kalyani is as follows:

ASCENDING: Sa Re Ga ma Pa Dha Ni Sa
DESCENDING: Sa Ni Dha Pa ma Ga Re Sa

2. Ragamallika: Ragamallika is the Carnatic equivalent of the north Indian ragamala. The ragas played here within the ragamallika are Satyapriya, Desh and Ramapriya. The frameworks of these ragas are as follows:

Satyapriya

ASCENDING: Sa Ga Ma Pa ni Sa

DESCENDING: Sa ni Pa ni dha Pa Ma Ga Pa Re Sa

Desh

ASCENDING: Sa Re Ma Pa Ni Sa

DESCENDING: Sa ni Dha Pa Ma Ga Re Ni Sa

Ramapriya

ASCENDING: Sa re Re ma Pa Dha Ni Sa

DESCENDING: Sa Ni Dha Pa ma Ga re Sa

i.e. on ascent Re appears to be both komal and shuddha. On descent Re is komal, Ma is tivra.

CHAPTER 28

Maharajapuram V. Santhanam

1928 – 1992

Maharajapuram V. Santhanam was the son of Maharajapuram Viswanath Iyer, one of the legends of Carnatic music. This great jewel of India started his musical career at an early age and was the sixth generation in the parampara of Saint Thyagaraja. He commanded supreme in the music world for over five decades and was one of the most popular names in vocal music. He created a style of his own that was a combination of rules and aesthetics. Interestingly, he was posted as a principal of Ramanathan Academy in Jaffna, Sri Lanka, for a period of time. Maharajapuram Santhanam received numerous awards and decorations through his glorious career including the

Sangeetha Sudhakara in 1955, Sangeetha Chudamani by Sri Krishna Gana Sabha, Kalaimamani by the government of Tamil Nadu, Mathura Kala Praveena by Sri Satguru Sangeetha Samajam, Madurai, Sur Singar by Sur Singar Samsad, Bombay, in 1987, Sangit Natak Academy Award in 1985, Sangitha Kalanidhi in 1989, Padmashri in 1990 and the Haafiz Ali Khan Award in 1991.

He was the Asthana Vidwan of Thirumala Tirupati Devasthanam, Kanchi Kamakoti Peetam, Shri Venkateswara Temple in Pittsburg, USA, and the Asthana Vidwan for the government of Tamil Nadu from 1984 to 1987.

He followed the path of his father Maharajapuram Viswanatha Iyer who was a veteran Carnatic singer. He was also a disciple of Melattur Sama Dikshitar. Maharajapuram Santhanam was a great composer. He wrote many songs on Lord Murugan and His Holiness Sri Chandrasekarendra Saraswati Swamigal (Maha Periyavar). His school of music was known as the Umayalpuram school.

We have met Santhanamji only a few times. The first was in Rani Sethai Hall in Chennai in 1988 at the Haafiz Ali Khan Award ceremony. The next was in 1992, when he received the Haafiz Ali Khan Award in New Delhi. He visited our residence the next day. Our father was planning an extravagant festival with him in New Delhi at Siri Fort auditorium, called 'Tribute to Tansen and Thyagaraja' the following year. However, this was not to be as Santhanamji died in a car crash the same year.

THE RECORDING

ALBUM: Maestros Choice, Maharajapuram V. Santhanam

TRACKS: Sankari Samkuru- Raga Saveri, Rama Ninu Nammina- Raga Mohanam, Himagiri Tanaye- Raga Suddha Dhanyasi, Padasanati Munijaja- Raga Kambhoji, Ehi Annapurne-Punnagavarali, Shanmukhan Bhaja- Raga Sindhu Bhairavi

ACCOMPANISTS: Nagai Muralidharan (violin) Thiruvarur Bhaktavatsalam (mridangam)

RELEASED BY: Music Today (1991)

1. Sankari Samkuru

Raga: Saveri
Tala: Adi, Tisra Gati
Composer: Shyama Shastri

A legendary composition of the great Shyama Shastri, this song is set in adi tala but in the tisra gati.

2. Rama Ninu Nammina

Raga: Mohanam
Tala: Adi
Composer: Thyagaraja.

The evergreen Raga Mohanam is presented in this composition by Thyagaraja. Since Carnatic music is text oriented, it is very important for the artiste to understand the essence of the text in order to deliver it, a task that Santhanam achieves perfectly.

3. Himagiri Tanaye

Raga: Suddha Dhanyasi
Tala: Adi
Composer: Muthayya Bhagavatar

Muthayya Bhagavatar was a great composer of his time. Many different types of varnams, kritis and tillanas were composed by him. He mainly composed in Telugu, Tamil, Sanskrit and Kannada.

4. Padasanati Munijana

Raga: Kambhoji
Tala: Misra Chapu
Composer: Swati Tirunal

Kambhoji is a very popular Carnatic raga and this extraordinary kriti was composed by Swati Tirunal, the maharaja of the state of Travancore.

5. Ehi Annapurne

Raga: Punnagavarali

Tala: Adi

Composer: Muthuswami Dikshitar

Muthuswami Dikshitar was the youngest of the Carnatic music composer trinity of Thyagaraja, Muthuswami Dikshitar and Shyama Shastri.

6. Shanmukham Bhaja

Raga: Sindhubhairavi

Tala: Misra Chapu

Composer: Swami Dayanand Saraswati

A moving bhajan in honour of Lord Subrahmanya concludes the great work of Santhanamji.

CHAPTER 29

M.L. Vasanthakumari

1928 – 1990

Affectionately and popularly known as MLV, Madras Lalitangi Vasanthakumari was the youngest recipient of one of Carnatic music's greatest honours, the Sangita Kalanidhi. MLV completed the female trinity of the greatest Carnatic singing divas, along with D.K. Pattamal and M.S. Subbulakshmi.

MLV was born to parents who were artistes of very high calibre. Her father Kuthanur Ayya Swamy Iyer and mother Lalithangi were instrumental in popularizing the compositions of the great Purandaradasa in south India. On hearing a young MLV, the legendary vocalist and one of the most prominent composers of recent decades, G.N. Balasubramaniam,

MLV with her disciple Sudha Ranganathan

took her under his tutelage. In fact, she was his first disciple. In time, MLV became an acclaimed singer in India and her music was described as sheer magic. Her imagination was unusual and her technique and skill excellent. Her renderings of ragas were unique and effortless. MLV was credited for further popularizing many compositions of Purandaradasa. Interestingly, one hears that she had learnt the subtle nuances of Raga Sindhu Bhairavi from Ustad Bade Ghulam Ali Khan sahib. This speaks great volumes of her open mindedness and greatness as an artiste.

We unfortunately never got a chance to meet the great MLV, but we spent some memorable moments with one of her senior disciples, the wondrous Sudha Raghunathan, during a tour that we shared in South Africa in 1995.

Grace and humility were part and parcel of this singing queen's persona. She was also a brilliant playback singer and sang for many films like *Manamagal*, *Raja Desingu*, *Or Iravu* and others that made her a household name. She received the Padma Bhushan in 1977 and a doctorate from Mysore University in 1976. A dream, a diva and a musician whose work provides a far better introduction than words can.

THE RECORDING

ALBUM: Akashvani Sangeet M.L. Vasanthakumari, Volume 1

ACCOMPANISTS: Sudha Raghunathan (vocal support), A. Kanyakumari (violin), T.S. Krishnanmurthy Rao (mridangam), K.M. Vaidyanathan (ghatam), G. Harisankar (khanjira)

RECORDED: 1980

RELEASED BY: All India Radio from the Akashvani Archives (2006)

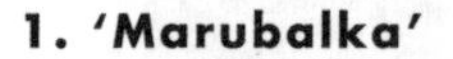

1. 'Marubalka'

Raga: Sriranjani

Tala: Adi

Sriranjini, as the name suggests, is a raga that pleases the goddess Lakshmi. This is very close to Raga Bageshri of Hindustani music. Compositions are rendered in the beginning of a concert in brisk tempo. Marubalka is an important and very popular kriti of Thyagaraja which is traditionally sung at the beginning of concerts with improvised svaras.

2. 'Saranam Bhava'

Raga: Hamsavinodini

Tala: Rupakam

This is a rare raga, which deletes Pa and is the offshoot of the Dheereshankarabharanam mela. Very few compositions have been composed by some minor composers and none by the trinity.

3. 'Manasaaramatyani'

Raga: Saramati

Tala: Adi

Saramati is a sampoorna-audava janya raga of Natabhairavi mela, deleting Pa and Re in the avarohana, the descent. The present kriti is a composition by Tanjore Sankaraiyyar though the most popular composition in this raga is Thyagaraja's 'Mokshamugalada'.

4. 'Ragam Tanam Pallavi'

Raga: Madhyamavati

Tala: Misra Chapu

As this track reveals, MLV has carved a niche for herself in the rendering of RTP.

A hallmark compilation of recordings of the great M. L. Vasanthakumari from her All India Radio broadcasts. Each and every track speaks volumes for itself. She is accompanied by some of the most renowned artistes like Sudha Raghunathan who was her disciple, the great khanjira exponent Hari Sankar and, of course, the violin genius A. Kanyakumari.

CHAPTER 30

Mogubai Kurdikar

1904 – 2001

One of the greatest vocalists this country has ever seen, Mogubai Kurdikar epitomizes the purity of music. Often called 'Gaana Tapasvini' by music enthusiasts, she was one of the foremost representatives of Ustad Alladiya Khan's Atrauli-Jaipur gharana. She learnt from the great ustad, as well as his brother Haider Ali Khan. When she grew older, she also trained under Ustad Bashir Khan and Ustad Vilayat Hussain Khan of the Agra gharana.

Mogubai Kurdikar was born on July 15, 1904, in the village of Kurdi in Goa. As a young girl, she joined two drama companies where she excelled as a child artiste and also got musical guidance from Chintopant

Mogubaiji with our family at Nehru Centre, Mumbai in January 1994

Gurav and Balkrishna Parwatkar. She also learnt Kathak dancing from Pandit Ram Lal. Mogubai's passion for Hindustani classical music took her to Sangli in 1919, where she started training under Inayat Khan Pathan. She also had intense training in laya, taal and tabla from Laya Bhaskar Khaprumama Parwatkar. This added a new dimension to her interpretation of layakari. A highly disciplined musician and a purist, Mogubai was uncompromising in her gharana principles. Taking Alladiya Khan sahib's musical legacy forward, she displayed sheer genius in her presentation of taan and boltaan patterns, and layakari.

We had the good fortune to meet this veteran singer in Mumbai in 1993 when she received the Haafiz Ali Khan Award at the Nehru Centre in Mumbai. She was almost childlike in her expressions and made the entire audience feel emotional as she received the award. She blessed both of us that day and also attended her daughter Kishori Amonkar's recital after the award ceremony. Both of us felt very blessed to have her in the audience when we gave our debut recitals at the same venue the next day.

THE RECORDING

ALBUM: Vintage 78 RPM Records Gaana Tapasvini Mogubai Kurdikar
RAGAS: Alhaiya Bilawal, Shukla Bilawal, Hindol, Nayaki Kanhara, Suha, Bageshwari, Multani, Purvi, Yaman, Kedar, Savani Kalyan and Jaijaiwanti
RE-RELEASED BY: Saregama (2005)

1. **Raga Alhaiya Bilawal:** 'Kahe Lajai Re Piya'

2. **Raga Shukla Bilawal:** 'Aao Aaj Baje Bajaye'

3. **Raga Hindol:** 'Chanak Mund Bhailava'

4. **Raga Nayaki Kanhara:** 'Mero Piya Rasiya'

5. **Raga Suha:** 'Pana Viri Main Kab Udini'

6. **Raga Bageshwari:** 'Tarana' (Pancham Sawari based in 15 beats)

7. **Raga Multani:** 'Haare Man Ka'

8. **Raga Purvi:** 'Aavan Kaye'

9. **Raga Yaman:** Composition in 15 ½ beats

10. **Raga Kedar:** 'Payo More Rama Naam Dhan'

11. **Raga Savani Kalyan:** 'Dev Dev Sant Sang'

12. **Raga Jaijaiwanti:** 'Aali Piya'

There is an unsurpassed magic in Mogubai's voice, heightened by complete fireworks, in this recording that was done in the peak of her career. Along with the scintillating taans, there is an interesting use of Pancham Sawari, a fifteen beat time cycle in Track 6, and a composition in 15 ½ beats in Track 9, something extremely unusual in vocal music.

CHAPTER 31

M.S. Subbulakshmi

1916 – 2004

It has been our good fortune to have met and shared some wonderful moments with M.S. Subbulakshmiji. Our relationship with her goes back a long way, perhaps to the time when we were not even born. Our mother, who was earlier known as Rajyalakshmi, was renamed Subhalakshmi after this great singer after our grandparents saw the film *Meera* in which she had acted. (Acting was always a fascination with classical musicians. While some did it, some didn't).

The first time we met Amma, as she was affectionately called, was in 1989 at Rani Sethai Hall in Chennai, when she was receiving the Haafiz Ali Khan Award. Her award was presented to her by her own

guru, Sangeet Pithama Semmangudi Srinivasa Iyer. During the same visit, she very kindly arranged our visit to Kanjipuram to take blessings from His Holiness Sri Chandra Sekharendra Saraswathi Swamigal, also called Periyavar. We were very fortunate to have darshans of all the three Shankaracharyas.

We met Amma again in 1995, once again at Narada Gana Sabha for our father's fiftieth birthday celebrations. She had come with Semmangudi Srinivasa Iyer and D.K. Pattammal. Sadly, all three of them are no more today. We also visited her home at that time and she was her charming self, as always full of radiance and positivity. She was the first Indian artiste to receive the Bharat Ratna in 1998.

The last time we met Amma was in Chennai at her residence in 2002. By this time she had become almost childlike in her ways. She had lost her husband and his death affected her health immensely. She felt her life was indebted to him, both spiritually and professionally. As for us, we will always value and cherish all those timeless moments we spent with her. She was a true devi and an example that Goddess Saraswati sent for the world to see and hear.

THE RECORDING

ALBUM: Sri Venkatesa Suprabhatam
Morning Shlokas by M.S. Subbulakshmi

TRACKS: Shri Venkatesa Suprabhatam, Bhavayami, Sri Rangapura Vihara

ACCOMPANISTS: R.S. Gopalakrishnan (violin), T.K. Murthy (mridangam)

RELEASED BY: Saregama (2004)

1. Shri Venkatesa Suprabhatam

It is needless to mention that Tirupathi is one of the greatest spiritual and pilgrimage centres in the world today. Amongst the many devotional songs and hymns in praise of Lord Venkatesa, Shri Venkatesa Suprabhatam is the most widely known and sung by devotees. To wake Lord Venkatesa, Suprabhatam is sung at dawn as an invocation. The hymn is based on 29 stanzas and opens with a shloka from Valmiki's Ramayana. According to traditional belief, this was the same shloka that was recited by Vishwamitra to wake Rama. In essence, the shloka describes a moment when all the sages, saints, devas and lords have assembled to wake up Lord Tirupathi. The Shri Venkatesa Stotra that comprises 11 shlokas is recited in a rhythmic frenzy. This is followed by the Shri Venkatesa Prapati which has a total of 16 stanzas and is an outpouring of dedication that the devotee makes at the lotus feet of Tirupathi. The hymns conclude with the Mangalasasanam, which is an auspicious hymn with 14 stanzas. The great M.S. Subbulakshmi presents the four traditional hymns in the authentic and traditional manner in which it has been sung at Tirupathi for years.

2. Bhavayami

Raga: Ragamalika
Tala: Rupaka
Composition: Swati Tirunal

Bhavayami is sung as a ragamalika made up of seven ragas: Saveri, Natakuranji, Danyasi, Mohanam, Mukhari, Poorvikalyani and Madhyamavati. They are beautifully woven into a song portraying the story of the Ramayana. This is a composition of Swati Tirunal (1813–1846) of Kerala, who was a great composer in the same period as the trinity of Tyagaraja, Muthuswami Dikshitar and Shyama Shastri.

3. Sri Rangapura Vihara

Raga: Brindavana Saranga
Tala: Rupaka
Composition: Muthuswami Dikshitar

Sri Ranagapura Vihara is a composition of Muthuswami Dikshitar. It is song in worship of Lord Parimala Ranga of Terazhundur in Tanjore. The accompanying artistes are R.S. Gopalkrishnan on the violin and T.K. Murthy on the mridangam. Both artistes were great names in their fields and add colour and magic to this timeless recording.

CHAPTER 32

Pandit Nikhil Banerjee

1931 – 1986

One of the greatest names in the world of sitar, Pandit Nikhil Banerjee lives on through his work and his disciples even after his premature death in 1986. An artiste who won great acclaim for the purity of his classical style and the vitality of his improvisations, he was a much loved musician and was always invited to the top music festivals. He travelled extensively and was a frequent performing artiste in Europe and the US. He was a true representative of his school of playing.

Nikhil Banerjee received his first lessons from his father, the well-known sitarist Shri Jitendranath Banerjee, and won acclaim at the early

Pandit Nikhil Banerjee with Pandit Kishan Maharaj, Kolkata 1973

age of nine at the All Bengal Sitar Competition. For five years thereafter, he learnt from Birendra Kishore Roy Chowdhury who then introduced him to the renowned Ustad Allauddin Khan. For the next seven years, he moved to Maihar and learnt both from Ustad Allauddin Khan and his son Ustad Ali Akbar Khan. He began touring abroad as early as 1955 and played in Australia, China, Nepal, Afghanistan, Russia, the east European countries and the US.

He participated in many memorable sarod-sitar duets with Ali Akbar Khan and was perhaps the only other sitarist that Ali Akbar Khan sahib performed with, as his musical partnership was usually with Pandit Ravi Shankar. Pandit Banerjee also used to teach every year at the American Society for Eastern Arts Summer School in Berkeley, California.

THE RECORDING

ALBUM: Immortal Sitar of Pandit Nikhil Banerjee

RAGAS: Purabi Kalyan, Zila Kafi and Kirwani

ACCOMPANISTS: Anindo Chatterjee (tabla) and Ratan Mukherjee (tanpura)

RELEASED BY: Chhanda Dhara (mid 1980s)

1. Raga Purabi Kalyan: Raga Purabi Kalyan was always a bit of a mystery. Different artistes laid claim to it, insisting that they had created the true version. But in reality, it was the Bisnupur school's version of Raga Purvi, also patronized by Ustad Dabir Khan and Ustad Wazir Khan of the Tansen family. It also inspired Rabindranath Tagore who used these notes in his song 'Aji e anondo shondha'. Basically, the notes of Puriya Kalyan are used with a shuddha madhyam. Nikhil Banerjee plays an exquisite alaap, with some great work in the kharajh strings, establishing the beautiful pure madhyam in this raga. The composition is set in teentaal. Some great improvisations are heard, along with some fabulous tabla solos by Anindo Chatterjee. The track ends with a very interesting tihai that is played together with the tabla.

2. Raga Zila Kafi: Raga Zila Kafi is mainly played by artistes in the lighter forms of classical music, though it can take a very traditional and serious form, too. One hears a very playful composition by Nikhil Banerjee here.

3. Raga Kirwani: The album ends with the ever popular Raga Kirwani from the south Indian system of classical music. The notes are the same as the harmonic minor scale in Western classical music. A slow composition is played to teentaal, followed by a fantastic climax.

CHAPTER 33

Pandit Omkarnath Thakur

1897 - 1967

His was one of the most influential names in the world of vocal music in his time. He is perhaps the only artiste who authored books on music of that era. He travelled in style and had a large number of admirers.

Orphaned at fourteen, Omkarnath Thakur went through an intense struggle in his search for the refinement of music. He was a disciple of Vishnu Digambar Paluskar. He was a master of his work, his musical approach unconventional and controversial. This was also why he had an incredible impact on people. He died in 1967, around the same time that he had announced his retirement from active concert life due to political reasons. He was awarded the Padmashri in 1955. He was also a recipient of awards like Sangeet Prabhakar and Sangeet Martand (Kolkata, 1940), and Sangeet Mahamahodaya (awarded by the ruler of Nepal in 1930). He was also closely involved with Sri Kala Sangeet Bharati in Banaras Hindu University from the year of its commencement in 1950.

During the freedom struggle, Omkarnath Thakur's 'Vande Mataram' was an integral part of the annual sessions of the Indian National Congress. He travelled to Italy in 1933 to participate in the International Music Conference in Florence. Today, he has a coveted representation in the music world through his most senior disciple, the violinist Srimati N. Rajam.

THE RECORDING

ALBUM: Golden Milestones Pt. Omkarnath Thakur
RAGAS: Todi, Desi Todi, Deshkar, Sughrai, Tankeshri, Tilang Thumri, Nilambari, Champak, Shuddha Kalyan and Shuddha Nat
RE-RELEASED BY: Saregama (2003)

Pandit Omkarnath Thakur had a beautifully cultivated and powerful voice. His singing had an emotional and dramatic effect and his fluent lecture-demonstrations were very popular. In fact, many of his recordings present him both singing and speaking. This is a very special recording as he performs several ragas that are rarely heard today.

1. Raga Todi: 'Garwa Main Sang Laagi'
A very traditional structured composition is sung. The usage of the Pa (5th note) is extremely aesthetic. Some lightning taans are heard at the end of the track.

2. Raga Desi Todi: 'Kadam Ki Chhaya'
Certain ragas of Indian classical music simply cannot be taught merely as an ascending and descending scale. There are ragas like Desi Todi that need to be understood, realized and felt. One has to go beyond the notes and understand the nature and atmosphere required by the raga. Omkarnath Thakur performs it to perfection with his signature elements.

3. Raga Deshkar: 'Jhanjariya Jhanke'
The traditional and now rare Raga Deshkar is given the most appropriate execution here. The strong characteristics of this raga stand out beautifully against the artiste's genius canvas.

4. Raga Sughrai: 'Mai Kanth Morwa'
The composition in Sughrai is a fast one set in teentaal. Lightning taans are heard by this legendary artiste.

5. Raga Tankeshri: 'Malan Laaye Chun Chun Kaliyan'
This is a rather rare raga of choice and the artiste presents two compositions in it. Its basic notes are the same as those of Raga Shree but here the 5th note is very prominent and the sharp 4th note is used in very small measure.

6. Tilang Thumri: 'Nanadiya Kaise Neer Bharun'
Raga Tilang is a very ancient raga that has been a favourite of most senior artistes. Although it is also played as a main raga, here it is sung as a thumri. The timeless movement of the notes 'Ga Ma Pa Ni Sa ni Pa Ga Ma Ga' sounds divine in the voice of Omkarnath Thakur.

7. Raga Nilambari: 'Mitwa Balamwa'
Yet another rare raga, Nilambari has the same notes as Raga Kafi. It is a raga that is almost unheard today. The movement 'Dha ni ga Re' is a prominent feature in this raga.

8. Raga Champak: 'Ae Mag Jai Ho'
Champak is another raga that has almost disappeared from music performances today. The notes are very close to the more popular Jhinjhoti.

9. Raga Shuddha Kalyan: 'Bolan Laage Nanadiya'
A very colourful Shuddha Kalyan is sung by the great artiste. This track can move a listener to tears solely by its appeal and effect.

10. Raga Shuddha Nat: 'Kahat Ho Mose'
A fitting finale to this album is the rendering of Shuddha Nat by Omkarnath Thakur. The raga is maintained to perfection. This raga has family ties with many ragas of the same notes and similar movements, but the raga stands on its own with its distinctive features and Omkarnath Thakur does full justice to it.

CHAPTER 34

Begum Parveen Sultana

1950 -

One of the things that makes it very easy for us to get along with Parveenji is that she belongs to Assam where our mother Subhalakshmi Khan is from, so we can speak to her in Assamese. Parveen Sultana is one of India's greatest singing gems. She is an artiste who believes in strict practising and who maintains that only practice can make you musically brilliant. When one hears her, you can sense sheer magic and exuberant energy. The power in her voice is limitless and the appeal uncanny. Her voice reaches the three octaves with effortless ease and grace.

Her first guru was her revered father Ikramul Majid. She also learnt from her grandfather Mohammed Najeef Khan. After this, she went to Kolkata and became a student of Pandit Chinmoy Lahiri. Finally, she started learning from her husband Dilshad Khan, who also happens to be sarodist Buddhadev Dasgupta's brother.

We first met Parveenji in 1993 in New Delhi at the Talkatora Stadium where she was singing after us for the Spirit of Freedom concerts for National Integration. It was a very brief meeting. We remember it was an early afternoon concert and it was evening by the time we got off stage. We then met her in Agra in 1999 where Zee TV was shooting classical musicians in performance with the Taj Mahal as the backdrop for their popular television show *Saregama* (which we were to host in the few years to follow). The next time we met Parveenji was in 2002 in Puttaparthy at Satya Sai Baba's birthday celebrations. She was very happy to hear us and blessed us after our concert. As an artiste, she is her own person and has made a name for herself that very few female vocalists could obtain and create. A true sultana of her music!

THE RECORDING

ALBUM: The Greatest Hits of Begum Parween Sultana
RAGAS: Ahir Bhairav, Shuddha Sarang, Nandkauns, Hori Thumri, Bramhanand Bhajan and Sadra Bhairavi
ACCOMPANISTS: Nizamuddin Khan, Anindo Chatterjee and Abhijit Banerjee (tabla), Vasanti Mhap Sekar, Mohammed Dhaulpuri and Shantaram Jadhav (harmonium)
RELEASED BY: Saregama (2008)

This recording by Saregama is a compilation of her great works and has an unconventional title for a classical music album — *The Greatest Hits of Parween Sultana.*

1. Raga Ahir Bhairav (1975):

Khayal in vilambit ektaal 'Sajan Aesi Ban Aaye'
Khayal in drut teental 'Mohe Chhedo Na Giridhari'
Harmonium: Vasanti Mhap Sekar
Tabla: Ustad Nizamuddin Khan

The timeless morning raga Ahir Bhairav is sung in the most appealing and effective manner. The prominent 'ni Sa Dha ni re' is presented with utmost beauty.

2. Raga Shuddha Sarang (1986):

Khayal in vilambit ektaal 'Dayanidhi Deen Saran'
Khayal in drut teentaal 'Tore Bina Nahi Chainva'
Harmonium: Mohammed Dhaulpuri
Tabla: Anindo Chatterjee

The most popular afternoon raga, Shuddha Sarang is still widely performed by musicians and enjoyed by music lovers, though there are very few afternoon concerts now. The raga has the usage of both the 4th notes (Ma), flat and sharp. The aesthetic usage needs appeal and vision, both of which we have here in abundance.

3. Raga Nandkauns (1975):

Khayal in vilambit ektaal 'Vyakul Nainan Neer Bahayen'
Khayal in drut teental 'Paddon Tore Main Paiyan'
Harmonium: Vasanti Mhapsekar
Tabla: Ustad Nizamuddin Khan

One of the most appealing ragas from the Kauns family of night ragas (like Malkauns, Jogkauns, Chandra Kauns, etc.), this raga was popularized by Parveen Sultana's guru Chinmoy Lahiri. In fact, this is a raga that our father borrowed from Chinmoy Lahiri and started playing in the sixties as he found it could be beautifully rendered on the sarod, too. The 3rd note (Ga) is used in both flat and sharp, creating an effect that is at once moving and majestic. As in all the tracks, Parveen

Sultana touches all three octaves with effortless ease along with lighting taans, gamaks and sargams.

4. Hori Thumri (1986):

Raga: Mishra Kafi 'Kaisi Kari Barajori Shyam'
Harmonium: Mohammed Dhaulpuri
Tabla: Anindo Chatterjee

This is a seasonal raga that celebrates the Holi festival. This particular rendition shows a combination of technical expertise and a creative imagination.

5. Bramhanand Bhajan (1994):

'Mere Matiya'
Harmonium: Shantaram Jadhav
Tabla: Abhijit Banerjee

Composed by Parveen Sultana's guru and husband, Dilshad Khan, this is a soulful rendition of a bhajan and is sung with depth and pathos.

6. Sadra Bhairavi (1975):

'Bhavani Dayani' in jhaptaal
Harmonium: Vasanti Mhap Sekar
Tabla: Ustad Nizamuddin Khan

The recording concludes with the beautiful Sadra Bhairavi. This is a raga whose basic scale uses all seven notes in their flat intonation (equivalent to the E-mode, or Prygian mode of Western classical music). A soulful interpretation by this great artiste of our times!

CHAPTER 35

Ustad Rais Khan

1939 –

Ustad Rais Khan was born into an old musical family in Indore, descended directly from the court musicians of the fifteenth century. His father Ustad Mohammad Khan initiated him into the art at a very young age. In his hands, the sitar sings in the style of an accomplished vocalist, reflecting the unique style of his playing.

Rais Khan sahib and our father knew each other well as they had played some duets in the years 1963 and '64. After Rais Khan moved to Pakistan in 1984, they lost touch. We first heard Rais Khan sahib perform in the Royal Festival Hall, London, where he played a duet

Ayaan, Ustad Rais Khan, Amaan and Farhan Khan, Kolkata 1996

with Sultan Khan. They played Charukeshi, a Carnatic raga, and were accompanied by Anindo Chatterjee and Sabir Khan.

After this, we met him in 1996 in Kolkata at a private concert. Private baithak concerts were once a very common feature in India but are now a bygone chapter. Rais Khan's son Farhan played on his own at the start of the concert and played a splendid Yaman. Following this, Rais Khan sahib played Raga Maru Behag followed by Shankara Behag, his own creation.He was once again accompanied by Sabir Khan on the tabla. This was the first time we interacted with him properly. He was very sweet to us and happy with our progress. He told us some funny stories of our father and him in the sixties. Rais Khan often wore dhotis at his concerts. He somehow managed to convince our father to wear a dhoti at one of their concerts together, but Abba could not get up after the concert until the curtain was down because his dhoti had opened!

The next concert we heard was in the same year at the Siri Fort in New Delhi. He played to a packed hall as he was playing in New Delhi after fifteen years. Quite recently, after going through several medical problems, Khan sahib performed in 2009 at the Vishnu Digambar Jayanti in New Delhi after a gap of many years. He presented the most splendid Raga Vachaspati. His recovery from a double pneumonia was forgotten the moment he took centrestage as he sounded as he always did — full of fireworks. Even today, he maintains the informal setting of classical music on stage as it was many years ago. He announced halfway into the concert that day that his mother had passed away that morning in Mumbai but he was keeping his commitment. As they say, 'the show must go on.'

Rais Khan also happens to be Vilayat Khan sahib's nephew, though they were never on good terms. As a sitarist, he is a trendsetter whose style is imitated even today.

THE RECORDING

ALBUM: Romantic Sound of the Sitar
RAGAS: Nand Kalyan, Shankara Behag and Dhun
ACCOMPANISTS: Zakir Hussain (tabla), Emam (tanpura)
RELEASED BY: Chhanda Dhara (1990)

1. Raga Nand Kalyan: The album opens with Raga Nand Kalyan. Traditionally, this raga is also known as Anandi or Anandi Kalyan. Khan sahib starts with the basic movement of the raga and then begins the vilambit composition. The raga unfolds very gradually with all its ornamentation and embellishments. A strong feature of this raga is the sequence of notes Ga Ma Dha Pa Re and it is very prominent in the composition. However, certain combinations of notes show the creative liberty of Rais Khan sahib. Towards the latter half of the track, he goes to the upper octaves just like a vocalist would go. Zakir uncle is as usual at his best and improvises only to complement Khan sahib's imagination further. One hears a lot of play with the rhythm, and embellishments in the typical Etawah gharana style, once the basic structure of the raga has been established. In earlier days, if an artiste and his style were popular, the style got the name of the region, city or area where he lived. For example, Etawah is the city in Uttar Pradesh where Imdad Khan, the patriarch of this school, lived.

2. Raga Shankara Behag: As the name suggests, Raga Shankara Behag is a combination of Behag and Shankara. Although the notes of both ragas are pretty much the same, the movements are quite different and very clearly outlined. The composition played is also an ideal cocktail of the two ragas. The legendary Rais Khan's speedy taans are at their creative best here. The use of gamaks and taans are beyond excellence and are followed by a superb jhala. Zakir Hussain once again performs some of his signature solos.

3. Dhun: The last track shows the true genius of Rais Khan where he plays a dhun based on a folk melody. Rais Khan sahib's years of playing for the Indian film industry for music directors like Madan Mohan and O.P. Nair have sitarists wanting to ape his style and tonal quality even today. His contribution to the sitar has been special, just as he is to the world of Indian classical music.

CHAPTER 36

Pandit Ravi Shankar

1920 -

Pandit Ravi Shankar is the man responsible for putting Indian classical music on the world map. Pandit Ravi Shankar made Indian classical music reach out to the mainstream audience in a way that no one else could. He became the true star of Indian classical music and introduced many new elements like solo evenings, programme notes and sound checks in the classical music industry. His collaborations have been pioneering and he has set very high standards for the Indian classical musician.

Ravi Shankarji came to our house in New Delhi in 1977 when Amaan was just three months old. After this, we met Baba, as he is

Panditji and his wife with our family, after our concert in memory of M.S. Subbulakshmi, New Delhi 2005

fondly called, in 1989 when he performed at Kamani Auditorium for Gandharva Mahavidyalaya in New Delhi. Gandharva Mahavidyalaya was established in 1939 by its founder-principal Shri Vinaya Chandra Maudgalya, a disciple of Pandit Vinayakrao Patwardhan. The institution's main objective was to commemorate the great Pandit Vishnu Digambar Paluskar, who was Vinayakrao Patwardhan's guru, and to popularize Indian classical music. The festival continues to take place today.

Baba was accompanied by Shafaat Ahmad Khan on the tabla and Durga Lal on the pakhawaj. After that, we have had the honour of meeting him and his family on numerous occasions. Our families are very fond of each other and though we are not constantly in touch, when we meet it is always memorable – full of humour, stories and industry gossip.

Some of the most memorable concerts that we attended of this master of the sitar were in 1989, 1991, 1995, 2000 and 2008 in New Delhi and in 2002 in Mumbai. We also remember attending his seventieth birthday celebrations at the Siri Fort auditorium in New Delhi in 1990. There was a short recital by Bismillah Khan sahib followed by songs sung by Anuradha Paudwal from some of the Hindi film scores that Pandit Ravi Shankar had composed.

We were very honoured to have visited Baba at his beautiful residence in San Diego in 2001. We were a bit late as our concert got over quite late but he was awake, waiting to receive us and have dinner with us. Even at this age, he performs hallmark concerts. He is a rare combination of the best of all worlds.

THE RECORDING

ALBUM: Sublime Sounds of Sitar, Pandit Ravi Shankar
RAGAS: Tilak Kamod, Bhatiyar and Dhun
ACCOMPANIST: Kumar Bose (tabla)
RELEASED BY: Oriental Records INC
PRODUCED BY: Rangasami Parthasarthy

1. Raga Tilak Kamod: Raga Tilak Kamod has always been associated with thumris and dadras and even when performed as the main raga, it has always been played in a lighter form. Conventionally, the opening raga needs to have a detailed alaap, establishing the character and the mood of the raga, followed by a jor and a jhala, and then compositions in various tempos. This would basically be termed as a main raga. A lighter raga would literally be like chocolate, dessert, after the main course!

Pandit Ravi Shankar's version of Tilak Kamod is perhaps the first of its kind where an extensive alaap, jor and jhala are played followed by a composition in dhamaar, a fourteen-beat cycle, and that too with a very complex rhythmic time cycle. Only a genius could think of this interpretation of Tilak Kamod.

Within the first few seconds of the start of the track, the atmosphere of the raga is created so effortlessly. Every raga commands a certain mood, a certain kind of handling and gravity. Although the rendition of a raga is indeed personal, certain phrases typically belong to that raga that establish it in no time.

The alaap establishes the beautiful features and framework of Tilak Kamod. The signature kharajh string of Panditji, tuned an octave lower than the keynote, of course does its magic as always. The jor section starts with the same level of grace and perfection. Some of the very popular phrases of Tilak Kamod are constantly heard in this section. As the tempo builds up, the adi chalan is played, followed by some amazing taan work along with some breathtaking 'beenkaar' syllable work which is a very significant feature of Panditji's style. The beenkar style was followed by all the members following the Senia Beenkar school of Ustad Wazir Khan,* who was Ravi Shankar's guru's guru. The composition in dhamaar has just the perfect flavour that this time cycle demands, with the most unpredictable and fantastic improvised tihais happening again and again. The tabla used here is called a kharajh tabla, which sounds more like a pakhawaj and gives the same effect. The pieces improvised by Kumar Bose are called paran baaj. The accompaniment is brilliant along with his solo pieces.

2. Raga Bhatiyar: Raga Bhatiyar is a very traditional morning raga, rarely played by instrumentalists. Panditji plays a beautiful vilambit composition and does a very relaxed improvisation establishing the raga and its frugal usage of the tivra madhyam (sharp 4th note). This is followed by some superb layakari with the off-beat musical notes playfully teasing the tabla rhythm, along with some thrilling tabla solo cycles by Kumar Bose. The track ends in the vilambit tempo itself.

3. Dhun: The last track in the album is a dhun composed by Panditji. It's a signature Ravi Shankar dhun. This is followed by an exciting tabla solo, a trend that he introduced in north Indian classical music where the tabla accompanist got full limelight. This is followed by a fast composition in teentaal based on the same notes. This finally climaxes with a crescendo and ends with a tihai.

* The school that was followed by the artistes who learnt under Ustad Wazir Khan of the Tansen family called it Senia Beenkar school as Wazir Khan was a been player.

CHAPTER 37

S. Balachander

1927 - 1990

Although he began his career as a sitar player, S. Balachander found his love and calling for the veena very quickly. Hence his passion, his life and his journey were dedicated to making the veena what it is today. In 1943, Balachander performed his inaugural concert on the veena. This was the dawn of a pioneering career. He developed a fresh movement, an innovative technique, a new discipline and a creative method of performing on the veena.

Sundaram Balachander was born in Chennai. In 1933, at the age of six, Balachander performed his first public concert, interestingly as a percussion accompanist on the kanjira. He also subsequently learnt to play the tabla. Since he was accomplished in both these instruments, he accompanied several vocalists including his elder brother S. Rajam, with whom Balachander performed extensively.

In the history of Carnatic music, Balachander made pioneering executions of his craft by performing entire concerts dedicated solely to melody, where instead of the traditional composition he played his music through alapana and taans, performing 45 ragas at once. This was played in sequence without a break. This extraordinary recital based on impromptu improvisations of 'unlimited' melody was remarkably performed without songs, words and accompaniments.

He was a staff-artiste in the Madras station of All India Radio and had the unique opportunity of playing and broadcasting on several other stringed and percussion instruments of Indian origin. He was a man of his principles. He was awarded the Padma Bhushan in 1982.

Although we never had the opportunity to meet Balachanderji, our father has a wonderful collection of his letters, which he used to write on very colourful stationery and in a very humorous way. Each letter was on a different coloured page and his signature resembled the veena, the love of his life.

THE RECORDING

ALBUM: S. Balachander, Veena
ACCOMPANISTS: Unknown
RELEASED BY: Saregama (2003)

The uniqueness of Indian classical music is that the south and north Indian systems are independent in nature and in presentation, even though they are based on the same twelve notes of music. Be it embellishments, techniques, concepts, usages or even ragas with similar or common names and notes, the colour and flavour are very distinctive.

As may be observed in the following recording of Dr Balachanderji, it is a very common trend in the Carnatic classical concert to present a vast repertoire of compositions which include ones that are very scholarly and others which are popular among music lovers and not limited to students of music. A concert may sometimes include as many as 12 to 14 compositions in different languages by different composers, which may feature all the musical forms of Carnatic music, both simple and intricate. The aim is to reach out to an audience which may comprise people speaking different languages.

The following recording includes several compositions, composed by the trinity, which are a must for concerts and also some popular Tamil, Telugu and Sanskrit compositions by composers of different southern states. The recording also includes the popular Hindi bhajan 'Raghupati Raghav'.

1. Mokshamu Galada

Ragam: Saramati
Tala: Adi
Composer: Thyagaraja

Mokshamu Galada is one of the most popular kritis in Raga Saramati composed by Thyagaraja. In fact, he has composed only one kriti in this raga and there are none by the other two of the trinity. The raga brings about a feeling of calmness and tenderness and is cherished by both performers and listeners.

2. Ninnuvinaga Mari

Ragam: Poorvikalyani
Tala: Chapu
Composer: Shyama Shastri

A very popular raga as which is elaborately rendered through RTP and kritis, giving scope for intricate alapana, niraval and kalpana svaras. A janya, or offshoot, of Gamanasrama mela, which corresponds to the Poorvi thaat of Hindustani music, it is close to Puriya Kalyan though it deletes Ni in the aroha. A popular raga even among composers, one can find many compositions by the trinity and other well-known composers like Swati Thirunal, Papanasam Sivan, etc. The kriti in this recording is one of the most popular compositions rendered in concerts.

3. Angarakam

Ragam: Curuti
Tala: Rupakam
Composer: Dikshitar

Dikshitar's compositions reflect Tantric worship in the Hindu pantheon. One can find compositions on panchalinga, panchabhuta, srividya, etc. Angarakam is one of the famous navagraha kritis, worshipping the planet Mars.

4. Raghuvamsa Sudhambudhi

Ragam: Kathanakuthoohalam
Tala: Adi
Composer: Patnam Subramania Iyer

This is a raga that adds lustre to a recital when rendered briskly and is therefore ideally suited for rendering after a long drawn-out composition like Angarakam. It is also suited for rendering tillanas. Patnam Subramania Iyer is noted for composing several madhyama kala compositions of which the present kriti is the most popular.

5. Naanina Dhyana

Ragam: Kanada
Tala: Chapu
Composer: Purandaradasar

Kanada is a popular raga in which one can find not only kritis but also varnams, padams, jawali and tillanas. This depicts the karuna rasa and is therefore ideally suited for depicting abhinaya, actions, in dance. In a tristhayi raga, the nuances are very subtle and the raga needs very careful and matured handling. Durbari Kanada of Hindustani music has some resemblance to this raga.

6. Smara Janaka

Ragam: Behag
Tala: Chapu
Composer: Swati Tirunal

Behag or Bihag is a popular Carnatic raga borrowed from Hindustani music. Swati Thirunal and Gopala Krishna Bharati were the first to adopt this raga in their kritis, 'smarajanaka' and 'adam chidambaram', respectively. Though borrowed from the north, the delineation is very different.

7. Sri Subramanyaya Namasthe

Ragam: Kambhoji
Tala: Rupakam
Composer: Muthuswami Dikshitar

Kambhoji, though a janya raga, is more popular than its mela raga Harikambhoji. Innumerable compositions have been composed by all well-known composers of the south. Each kriti composed by the trinity brings out a different colour of the raga. Sri Subramanyaya is a composition that is rendered to a slow rhythm and with difficult nuances and it needs expertise of the highest order for its correct and effective rendition, something that Balachander achieves to perfection.

8. Theruvil Varaano

Ragam: Khamas
Tala: Rupakam
Composer: Muthu Thandavar

Raga Khamas is a popular raga which is closer to Raga Khamaj of Hindustani music. This raga finds an important place in the realm of dance as it suits the depiction of sringara rasa. Unlike the Hindustani version of this raga, Khamas adopts both nishads.

9. Sarasamulaade

Ragam: Kapi
Tala: Adi
Composer: Ramanthapuram Srinivasa Iyengar

Kapi is a janya raga of Kharaharapriya mela which corresponds to the Kafi thaat. This is a popular raga and many padams, jawalis and padavarnams have been composed in this raga.

10. Aiyeh Metha Kadinam

Ragam: Ragamalika
Tala: Adi
Composer: Gopalakrishna Bharathi

11. Theerada Vilayattu Pillai

Ragam: Ragamalika
Tala: Adi
Composer: Subramania Bharati

Ragamalikas are rendered towards the end of a concert, to lighten the mood after the scholarly rendering of RTP. 'Theerada Vilayattu' is a very popular song by Subramania Bharati and is known even to those who don't have a keen ear for heavy classical music.

12. Raghupati Raghava

This timeless bhajan, also a favorite of Mahatma Gandhi, is played with the most mesmerizing interpretation by Balachander.

13. Thullumuda Vel Kai

Ragam: Hamsanandi
Tala: Adi
Composer: Arunagirinathar

Hamsanandi is a raga that resembles Raga Sohini of Hindustani music. Though some important composers have composed in this raga, one does not find any by the trinity.

14. Mangalam

Ragam: Sourashtram

Tala: Adi

Composer: Thygaraja

The recording ends with a mangalam.

CHAPTER 38

Pandit Samta Prasad

1921 – 1994

The matchless Pandit Samta Prasad of Varanasi is an exemplar of 'firework' tabla. Gudai Maharaj, as he was also known, was a soloist of the highest calibre and an accompanist of unusual sensitivity and technical skill. He was revered to the extent that when a concert was organized, he would be booked first and then the main artistes were approached. From Ali Akbar Khan to Amjad Ali Khan, Vilayat Khan to Ravi Shankar, they were all his admirers and fellow artistes at several timeless concerts.

Samta Prasad hailed from a renowned family of tabla players from the Benaras gharana. He was the son of Shri Shivsundar, Pandit Baccha

Maharaj, and the great-grandson of Shri Pratap Maharaj. His musical training began under his father and after his father's death his mother, who belonged to a famous family of musicians from the court of Benaras, brought him up. Pandit Samta Prasad led a simple life in Benaras but quickly became a monumental icon in the world of music.

His career was not restricted to classical concerts alone. Samta Prasad played for several films including *Jhanak Jhanak Payal Baje* (1955) and *Sholay* (1975). In 1972, he received the Padmashri for his outstanding contributions to the tabla and also received the Sangeet Natak Akademi Fellowship the same year. There was no tabla player who did not follow him or, for that matter, get influenced by his style. He died in Pune in 1994.

He was a simple man whose interests ranged from music to astrology. He enjoyed looking at charts and predicted things about his contemporaries. We are very fortunate to have not just met him but also performed with him. In 1992, he visited our house and we were blessed that we got the chance to play a little with him. That day, he advised us: Practice, and only practice. That's just the way it is. That is the mantra.

THE RECORDING

ALBUM: Pandit Samta Prasad
TRACKS: Tabla Solo in teentaal
ACCOMPANIST: Unknown (harmonium)
RELEASED BY: Atlantis Music (2001)

Samta Prasad had his own style of playing. He followed his own rules and his presentation was completely unconventional. In this recording, he presents a firework solo set entirely to teentaal.

The recording begins with an uthaan followed by a gat from the Benaras gharana. He also presents qaidas and baant from the Delhi school. The tirakit and dhirakit in his qaida create an atmosphere that almost sounds like a rela. He then presents some amazing versions of more interpretations from the Ajrara and Delhi schools of playing.

The relas are presented in slower and then faster versions as always and then the artiste recites and plays some gats composed by some great iconic names from the tabla world. Many technically challenging moments are captured in this recording including parans, qaida variations, relas and meend fards. A masterpiece not just for listeners of music but also for students of the tabla.

CHAPTER 39

Semmangudi R. Srinivasa Iyer

1908 - 2003

Semmangudi Srinivasa Iyer is famously known as the 'pitamaha' of Carnatic music. When we were children, he was one of the artistes who had the deepest impact on us. We were told by our father that he was a legendary figure in the Carnatic music world, but what really impressed us was that he stayed at Rashtrapati Bhawan with President R. Venkatraman in New Delhi when he came to receive the Haafiz Ali Khan Award in 1988. Needless to say, this childish impression turned somewhat sacred in the years to follow. We were very fortunate to meet him a number of times and also hear him live in Chennai in 1989. His simplicity was his trademark. He could never agree more when our father would suggest to him that the terms Hindustani and Carnatic should not be used as they create a division in the music world and that they should instead be called classical music of the north and classical music of the south.

Semmangudi Srinivasa Iyer was born into a musical family. The eminent violinist Tirukkodikaval Krishna Iyer was his maternal uncle. He started learning music at the age of eight from his cousin, the illustrious violinist Semmangudi Narayanaswamy Iyer. He later learnt under Gonu Vadhya Vidwan Tiruvidaimarudur Sakharama Rao for a few years and then from Sangeetha Kalanidhi Umayalpuram Swaminatha Iyer and in due course from Sangeetha Kalanidhi Maharajapuram Viswanatha Iyer.

The first music recital Semmangudi gave was in 1926. He was Asthana Vidwan of the Travancore Royal Court in 1939. In 1941, he joined the Sri Swati Tirunal College of Music in Trivandrum to complete, edit and put together the kritis of Maharaja Sri Swati Tirunal. After this, he became the principal of the college.

One of the greatest Carnatic vocalists that the twentieth century, or indeed any other age, has ever seen, Semmangudiji was the recipient of several awards including the Rajya Seva Niratha by the Maharaja of Travancore, Sangeetha Kalinidhi by the Madras Music Academy, Sangeetha Kala Ratna conferred by His Holiness Jagadguru Sankaracharya of Kanchi Kamakoti Peetham, the Kalidas Samman by the government of Madhya Pradesh and the Haafiz Ali Khan Award.

He has trained a generation of artistes including the legendary M.S. Subbulakshmi. We have both been very fortunate to have had this great icon of music in the audience at our debut concert in Chennai in 1993.

THE RECORDING

ALBUM: Semmangudi R. Srinivasa Iyer, Vocal

RAGAS: Begada, Ritigowla, Subhapantuvarali

ACCOMPANISTS: P.S. Narayanaswami (vocal support), T.N. Krishnan (violin), S.V.S Narayanan (mridangam)

RELEASED BY: Saregama (2003)

All India Radio recorded several illustrious musicians at the peak of their careers. In those days, the radio with its unparalleled reach was the ideal medium of broadcast. On completing 75 years, the All India Radio archives released many recordings under their label Akashvani Sangeet in association with Saregama. It is apt that Semmangudiji's recording should be re-released like this as he had a long and close association with the station. He performed at its inauguration in Chennai in 1938 and was also the chief producer of All India Radio in the 1950s.

This recording was made in the early sixties and stands testimony to Semmangudiji's genius. He performs four popular kritis that demonstrate his skill and musicianship of the highest levels.

1. Vallabha Nayakasya

Raga: Begada
Tala: Rupaka
Composer: Muthuswami Dikshitar

Raga Begada is an auspicious raga, sometimes sung at the beginning of a concert. Vallabha Nayakasya is a composition in praise of Lord Ganesha, the bestower of all desired boons. The melodic structure has intricate nuances which give the complete svaroopa of the raga.

2. Janani Ninuvina

Raga: Ritigowla
Tala: Misra Chapu
Composer: Subbaraya Sastri

Ritigowla is a scholarly tristhayi raga that portrays a feeling of pathos. The composition is a prayer offered to the goddess, regarded as the mother of three worlds, seeking her blessings and protection.

3. Sri Satyanarayanam

Raga: Subhapantuvarali
Tala: Rupaka
Composer: Muthuswami Dikshitar

Subhapantuvarali is a melakarta raga that corresponds to the Todi thaat of Hindustani music. Among the trinity, only Dikshitar composed in this raga and that too only one composition. Sri Satyanarayana is a fine blend of both Carnatic and Hindustani music as Dikshitar was a composer who travelled in the north and had a knowledge of both traditions of music.

CHAPTER 40

Pandit Shiv Kumar Sharma

1938 –

The true and only pioneer of the santoor, Pandit Shiv Kumar Sharma's role in getting the instrument into mainstream visibility is beyond definition. He is the first person to play Indian classical music on the santoor (originally a folk instrument), and every santoor player today and in years to come owes their musical career to this one man.

Shiv Kumar Sharma's musical knowledge was bequeathed to him by his father Pandit Uma Dutt Sharma, an extraordinarily learned musician from Jammu who was a disciple of Bade Ramdas of Benaras. Interestingly, before he started to play the santoor, this great artiste was a tabla player and he has accompanied many great musicians, right from Bhimsen Joshi to Ravi Shankar.

We first met Shiv uncle in 1989 during the ITC Sangeet Sammelan along with Hari Prasad Chaurasia, Zakir Hussain and Shafaat Ahmad Khan. After this, we attended many of his concerts, including the ITC Music Festival in New Delhi (1989), Rajiv Gandhi Foundation (1990) and the St Xavier's Music Festival in Mumbai (1992). We also remember a fantastic Gorakh Kalyan rendition by him in Gwalior at the Haafiz Ali Khan Music Festival in 1996.

Panditji's musical partnership with Pandit Hari Prasad Chaurasia is legendary. Together as music directors (the famous Shiv-Hari duo), they have delivered some timeless music for Hindi films like *Silsila*, *Chandni*, *Lamhe*, *Darr* and *Sahiba*. We have visited his residence on numerous occasions and it has always been memorable. Once, he was composing music for one of the films and he made us hear some of the recorded songs in his music room before they were released commercially.

Soft-spoken and elegant, Shiv uncle has always encouraged us as artistes, and we finally had the chance to perform in the same festival in 1994, along with our father, for the Rajiv Gandhi Foundation in New

Delhi. It is a humbling experience to now participate in festivals with these great artistes, in front of whom we grew up.

THE RECORDING

ALBUM: A Concerto in Raga Yaman, Indian Night Live Stuttgart '88
RAGA: Yaman
ACCOMPANISTS: Zakir Hussain (tabla), Shefali Nag (tanpura)
RELEASED BY: Chhanda Dhara (1990)

The album commences with a detailed and slow alaap. This was, perhaps, unthinkable at one point of time on the music scene. But when one hears Pandit Shiv Kumar Sharma's alaap on the santoor, one feels as though it was always meant to be played that way. After the raga has been beautifully established, the jor section begins with some groovy patterns, reaching a point of meditative bliss. As the tempo increases, the improvisation and the movements achieve an unreal frenzy. The track is summed up with an exhilarating jhala.

The alaap is based in chaar taal ki sawari, an eleven beat cycle. The most phenomenal layakari and offbeat patterns are played with effortless ease and imagination. Ustad Zakir Hussain responds with some breathtaking pieces on the tabla. The medium and fast compositions are set to teentaal. The entire recording can only be described as sheer magic.

CHAPTER 41

Shobha Gurtu

1925 – 2004

Shobha Gurtu came from a family in which music was worshipped. She received her initial lessons in music from her mother Menakabai Shirodkar, a noted dancer of her time, who also trained in vocal music in the Atrauli-Jaipur style of Ustad Alladiya Khan. Later, she had the opportunity to learn classical vocal from Nathan Khan and light classical and popular music from Ghamman Khan. Her father-in-law, Pandit Narayan Nath Gurtu, who was a scholar and a musician gave her valued guidance and direction in her artistic quest.

We first met Shobha Gurtuji in Gwalior in 1997; this was when she had come to receive the Haafiz Ali Khan Award. It was presented to her by Pandit Kishan Maharaj. She very sweetly referred to both of us as 'Baba'. The last time we met her was in 1997 in New York when she was part of India's 50th year of Independence celebrations at Carnegie Hall. She was one of the most sought after and respected thumri singers India had ever seen. She was affectionately called 'Thumri Queen' by the music-loving public.

THE RECORDING

ALBUM: The Genius of Shobha Gurtu
RAGAS: Kajri in Mishra Tilak Kamod, Thumri in Kafi, Thumri in Khamaj, Hori in Ghara, Dadra in Misra Sarang, Thumri in Jogia, Dadra in Bhairavi
ACCOMPANISTS: Nizamuddin Khan (tabla), Sultan Khan (sarangi), Purushottam Walavalkar (harmonium)
RELEASED BY: Universal (1983)

1. Raga Mishra Tilak Kamod: This recording of Shobha Gurtu is undoubtedly a collector's item; it captures the essence of the wonderful work that she did. The album opens with a kajri in Raga Mishra Tilak Kamod. The lyrics are 'Sawan Ki Ritu Aayee Ri'. Each and every moment of this album is perfect in its purity and musical quality.

2. Raga Kafi: The thumri in Kafi is 'Anchara Chodo Kanhai', usually sung during the festive time of Holi. The beauty of Raga Kafi seems to be literally painted on a canvas with colours of eternal beauty. Nizamuddin Khan sahib plays a phenomenal laggi at the end of this piece.

2. Raga Khamaj: Raga Khamaj is sung in a thumri form and the lyrics are 'Radha Nandkunwar Samjhaye'. The typical thumri elements are present here in embellishments and creativity. Sultan Khan sahib creates magic alongside Shobha Gurtuji.

4. Raga Ghara: The hori is based in Raga Ghara, the lyrics are 'Main To Kheloongi Unhi Se Hori'. The flavour of Raga Ghara is established in all its glory with a laggi at the end by Nizamuddin Khan sahib.

5. Raga Misra Sarang: 'Patjhad Aayee Sakhiyan' is the next track based on Misra Sarang. All ragas of the Sarang family are afternoon ragas. This piece is sung in dadra.

6. Raga Jogia: Jogia is a raga that is very popular amongst vocalists, always sung at the end of a concert like Bhairavi. The words here are 'Sakhiri Mora Maike Mein Jiya Ghabraye'.

7. Raga Bhairavi: The last song of this great album is in Raga Bhairavi. Set to dadra tempo again, it is a fitting finale. The words are 'Hamri Atariyape Aajare Sawariya'.

CHAPTER 42

T.R. Mahalingam

1926 – 1986

It is ironic that we write this chapter on Krishna Janmashtami as the legendary T.R. Mahalingam had acted in a Tamil film called *Nanda Kumar* in 1938 in which he played the role of Lord Krishna.

T.R. Mahalingam began to play the flute at the age of five. His first major performance was at the Thyagaraja Festival in Mylapore, Chennai, when he was just seven. Affectionately called Mali, he started learning vocal music under his uncle Jalra Gopala Ayyar. He researched extensively on classical music and received the National Award for excellence in music in 1965.

Latif Ahmed Khan, Malabika Kanan, Jasraj, Vijay Kitchlu, Amjad Ali Khan, T.R Mahalingam, Kishan Maharaj, Ghulam Mustafa Khan in Kolkata 1973

The style created by T.R Mahalingam was legendary. He fashioned a new technique of finger movement that made the flute sound almost like a human voice. His contribution has been unparalleled and impacts Carnatic flute players even today. He was a dynamic and skilled musician who would constantly think, innovate, and create new tunes. He was also trained in vocal music, and his training in breathing techniques helped in his quest to make the flute sing.

THE RECORDING

ALBUM: Akashvani Sangeet T.R. Mahalingam, Carnatic Flute

ACCOMPANISTS: M.S. Gopalkrishnan (violin), C.S. Muruga Bhoopathi (mridangam), M.N. Kandaswamy (khanjira), Alangudi Ramachandran (ghatam)

RELEASED BY: Akashvani (1962); re-released by All India Radio (2007)

1. **Sarasija Nabha Varnam**
   Kambhoji Khanda Ata
   Swati Tirunal
2. **Mivalia Kapi Khanda Chapu**
   Thyagaraja (5 Aksharaas)
3. **Ragam Tanam Pallavi, Kalyani**
   Mishrachapu (7 Aksharaas)

CHAPTER 43

Pandit V.G. Jog

1921 - 2004

Pandit V. G. Jog was by far one of the greatest violinists of north Indian music. He was a most adorable man, full of humility and great dignity, and his personality made him one of the most well-loved artistes of India. We also remember him for his interesting collection of kurtas, which were quite fancy! Panditji was born in Bombay in 1921, and trained under luminaries like S.G. Athavale, Ganpat Rao Purohit, V. Shastry and Dr. S.N. Ratanjankar. He even received guidance from Ustad Allauddin Khan for a short while. A master of ragas, his forte was his control over rhythm.

We met Panditji for the first time in New Delhi in 1990, the year our father played two duets with him. They had also played together in the early seventies in Berlin. One jugalbandi was played at the Siri Fort auditorium and the other was a recording for Doordarshan, India's only television channel at that time. We played the tanpura for both the performances, along with our father's student Shanti Sharma who is now no more. We clearly remember that the recording was a day after Ravi Shankar's 70th birthday celebrations, also held at the Siri Fort

Jog sahib, our father and Ayaan at the Sarod Ghar museum in Gwalior, November 1996

auditorum. Zakir uncle was to play at the recording the next day, but he had left for Muscat! However, Abba made arrangements for a backup tabla player. Jog sahib very affectionately familiarized us with his violin. Interestingly, he had put sympathetic strings on his instrument, which gave it a resonance similar to that one would get out of sympathetic strings on the sarod, sitar or sarangi.

We met Jog sahib once again when he received the Haafiz Ali Khan Award in Mumbai in 1994. In fact, in his speech he mentioned that he had learnt a little under our grandfather. We met him quite a few times in Kolkata at various concerts and functions. He was very kind to us and also attended many of our performances. We heard yet another memorable duet of Jog sahib and our father in Kolkata at Nazrul Mancha in 1996, which was a part of Jog sahib's 75th birthday celebrations.

The veteran violinist had travelled all over the world and won numerous awards and titles over his long musical journey. Unfortunately, he had a very sad end, when his health deteriorated and he also suffered many other personal crises. His son passed away during this time, but he was not told about it due to his own ill health. His demise was the end of yet another glorious chapter in Indian classical music.

THE RECORDING

ALBUM: Pandit VG Jog 75th Birthday Celebrations
RAGAS: Kirwani and Kajri
ACCOMPANIST: Zakir Hussain (tabla)
RECORDED: Live at Logan Hall in 1981
RELEASED BY: Navras Records (1996)

1. Raga Kirwani: Jog sahib presents the very popular south Indian classical raga Kirwani, which is set in the harmonic minor scale. Today, it has become one of the most popular ragas to be played by Indian musicians, both from the north and the south. The recording starts with a brief alaap that flows almost like a song. Interestingly, Jog sahib's approach and creativity almost execute the thought processes of a sarod or sitar player. He presents two compositions in Kirwani. The first composition is a slow one set to teentaal. Intricate taans, flashes of adi (a rhythmic pattern) and some anaaghat (a composition that ends before the sum, the first beat) improvisations are heard here. One can also hear the 'gayaki ang' or human voice effect very frequently. Zakir uncle accompanies him with great understanding and support.

The medium tempo composition is also set to teentaal. The amazing bow technique of Pandit Jog can be heard in this recording. He also strums a string constantly in continuity, creating an effect of chikari or drone strings. Some magical moments are created in this track with sawal jawab, brilliant taan patterns and the picking up of the composition from the seventh beat. Again, some great solos are played by Zakir uncle. The track ends at a very high speed. It is surreal to hear a jhala presented on the violin, an instrument that has no drone strings.

2. Kajri: The recording ends with a superb kajri from the city of Benaras. It is set to Keharwa, an eight beat time cycle. The tabla provides a great groove for the artiste to improvise freely. Jog sahib plays flashes of some interesting notes of Bhatiyali, Basant, Megh and Punjabi folk. There is a very interesting sawal-jawab session between the violin and tabla where Ustad Zakir Hussain answers only on the baayaa (the left drum). A great testimony to a great artiste, rightly released on the momentous occasion of his 75th birthday.

CHAPTER 44

Ustad Vilayat Khan

1928 - 2004

The legendary sitar maestro Vilayat Khan sahib needs little introduction. An instrumentalist who was a hero among his contemporaries, Ustad Vilayat Khan gave the sitar its current expressiveness and wide canvas. A child prodigy at the age of six and an Ustad in his own right in his teens, the world of Indian classical music had never heard or seen anything like him.

His father was Ustad Enayet Hussain Khan and his grandfather was Ustad Imdad Khan, both known for their musical genius. Unfortunately, Vilayat Khan lost his father very early in life, but this only made him more determined in his fanatical quest for musical excellence. He also

With Taaya Abba and our father in Dehradun

trained in vocal music under some great ustads and reproduced every vocal nuance on his sitar, a feature that stood out in his melodious and soulful playing. His maternal grandfather Bande Hasan Khan was a singer of high repute and Vilayat Khan also found influences for his musical expression from Ustad Mushtaque Hussain Khan of Rampur, Ustad Amir Khan (his one-time brother-in-law) and most importantly from Ustad Abdul Karim Khan of the Kirana gharana.

We can never forget the first time we met Vilayat Khan sahib. It was for lunch at his house in Dehradun, and we shall always remember it as the most amazing interaction we have ever witnessed between our father and another artiste. This was in 1987. The two of them discussed students, sang out compositions, exchanged musical ideas, and lunchtime went on till dinner. After this, we had countless meetings with Taaya Abba (as we called him) in New Delhi, Kolkata and in his residence in Princeton, New Jersey.

Vilayat Khan's death in 2004 marks the end of a glorious chapter in Indian classical music and sitar playing. The first time we heard him playing was at the Dover Lane Music Festival in Kolkata in 1990 where he played Raga Ramkali. This was followed by many more memorable performances, such as at the ITC Music Festival in New Delhi (1990) where he played Raga Sanjh Sarawali, his own creation, and then again his duet with Bismillah Khan for the Rajiv Gandhi Foundation at the Siri Fort auditorium in New Delhi in 1993. The two maestros played a raga called Purba, traditionally known as Puriya Kalyan, followed by Anandi and a ragamala. There was another memorable evening in New Delhi in 1994 when he played with Pandit Kishan Maharaj on the tabla for Raag Rang, a music festival that was started by the great thumri singer Naina Devi. That evening, Vilayat Khan sahib played Raga Gawoti and a ragamala. Even though there had been an outburst of plague in Delhi at that time, the hall was packed. The last time we met and heard Taaya Abba was at Dover Lane in 2002. He played a superb Raga Bihagada followed by a ragamala for which he got a standing ovation.

Vilayat Khan sahib was a man of principles and he lived his life according to his own terms. He had a phenomenal sense of humor and was also a great mimic. He was passionate about so many things in life, from good cars to fantastic shawls. He was very true to his craft, so much so that music could conquer his heart and mind in all situations in life. Indeed, he was special to all who knew him and understood him.

THE RECORDING

ALBUM: Raga Yaman
RAGA: Yaman
ACCOMPANIST: Manik Rao Popatkar (tabla)
RELEASED BY: Saregama (1968)

Raga Yaman is the evergreen and ever so beautiful evening raga. A raga that is usually the first raga a beginner would learn, a master's interpretation only humbles younger musicians. Raga Yaman in Vilayat Khan sahib's hand was like air in the atmosphere. Only natural!

ASCENDING: Ni Re Ga ma Dha Ni Sa
DESCENDING: Sa Ni Dha Pa ma Ga Re

The recording begins with a vilambit composition. In those days, to begin a performance without an alaap was very unconventional — but only geniuses take a stand. In any case, no book or shastra has ever declared that an alaap is a must before playing a composition. Khan sahib plays an elaborate piece, glorifying Yaman. At times, his sitar almost sounds as if someone is singing within. In fact, his sitar is known to have sounded on occasion like the voices of Ustad Bade Ghulam Ali Khan and Ustad Rajab Ali Khan, particularly when the maestro concentrated on intricate patterns. Manik Rao Popatkar gives wonderful support that makes the bouquets of musical notes sound even more beautiful. This vilambit composition of Khan sahib created a frenzy when he performed it on stage. So much so that the entire audience perhaps memorized it after this album was first released.

This is perhaps the only album in the history of Indian classical music where there are two kinds of vilambit compositions in the same raga and yet they have completely different flavours. The second track has a vilambit composition which is slightly higher in speed and plays with variations of tempo against a constant teentaal. He also plays some fine off-beat work along with his lightning taans. The tabla also plays some thrilling solos. This recording clearly shows how this man became the man he was and why he was one of a kind.

The album concludes with a drut composition that is one of Khan sahib's best compositions and became a superhit in its time. The mix of taan and bolbaat (a particular sequence of syllables on the right hand for instrumentalists) makes it all the more unique. The taans played here bring the house down. The concept of using the movement 'Sa Ga Re Ga' is entirely Khan sahib's interpretation of Yaman. The track ends with a scintillating jhala that inspired all instrumentalists no end then and does so even now. Truly a firework!

DUETS

CHAPTER 45

Ustad Alla Rakha and Ustad Zakir Hussain

Ustad Alla Rakha was born in 1919 in Phagwal, a village in Jammu. He did not come from a family of musicians and received his initial musical training from the great Mian Kader Baksh of the Punjab gharana in Lahore. Khan sahib also received vocal training from the great singer of the Patiala gharana, Ustad Aashiq Ali Khan. After moving to Mumbai, he quickly became a regular at all the Indian music festivals. He also composed music for many films as a music director under the name A.R. Qureshi (a surname that his other two sons, Fazal Qureshi and Taufiq Qureshi, continue to use). This great stalwart's legendary musical partnership with Pandit Ravi Shankar was

a renaissance in classical music around the world. It was Alla Rakha Khan sahib's genius that he also collaborated with many great artistes of the West including the legendary jazz drummer Buddy Rich. Alla Rakha Khan sahib was a symbol of simplicity and charm. His house in Mumbai was always open to his students and other artistes. He has been a patriarch of his field and his death on February 3, 2000, was a real shock to the music fraternity.

We are very fortunate to have met Khan sahib on numerous occasions. He was always warm, kind and blessed us immensely. We met him many times but the first time he came to our house was very memorable. We had gone to his concert at the Taj Palace hotel in New Delhi along with his son Zakir Hussain in 1993. After the concert, Khan sahib came home with us. Our family friend Rakhee Gulzar was also in our residence at that time. We also met him in Hyderabad in 1996 during the ITC Music Festival and a few times in Mumbai in the early nineties. We clearly remember that the last time we met him was in Ahmedabad in 1999 at the Saptak Festival. He played a tabla duet with his younger son, Fazal Qureshi, after which we had our duet. Abbaji, as he was fondly called, was sitting in the wings and blessed us from there with his beautiful smile and grace.

On the day he passed away, we were playing in Nagpur. Needless to say, the concert was dedicated to Ustad Alla Rakha. The next day we went to his residence which was filled with people. It is our great loss that we never got to play with him.

What can one say about Ustad Zakir Hussain? A man who redefined tabla and a son that every father should have, he is a skilled musician with a phenomenal following. Our first interaction with him was in 1984 in New Delhi. We had gone out for lunch with him and our family. The following evening, he played at the Siri Fort auditorium with the great Kathak dancer Durga Lal. After this, we met him in 1991 in Mumbai. He has very graciously accompanied us on numerous occasions from 1996 up to 2005, both in solo concerts and in duets and, of course, with our father. We have had the most memorable concerts in India, the United States and Australia. Zakir uncle is a sensitive and private human being and he is his own person. He was always an example our father would give not just in terms of the artiste he is but in the way he regards and respects other artistes.

THE RECORDING

ALBUM: Shared Moments Ustad Alla Rakha and Ustad Zakir Hussain

TRACKS: Vilambit Amad, Peshkar, Qaida and Chakradar Drut, Fast Tempo, Chakradars, Chalan and Tani Avartanam in Teentaal

ACCOMPANISTS: Ustad Sultan Khan (sarangi)

RELEASED BY: Navras Records, licensed from Musenalp (2004)

The recording is indeed a masterpiece because one sees the tradition of performance between father and son, guru and disciple. The concert begins with Sultan Khan sahib playing the most melancholic melody on the sarangi, after which the tablas take over once the naghma has been established. This track has the father-son duo present peshkars, tehais and qaidas. They are at their creative best and represent a powerhouse of knowledge and calibre.

In the vilambit tempo, the artistes present a series of chakradars which are recited and then played in different metrical canvases. The climax is performed in what is called a Tani Avartanam, a rhythmic exhibition from the south Indian world of percussion. This is followed by an exchange of numerous tihais and a powerful chakradar tihai as a crescendo.

Theirs was an iconic presentation. They continue to be the symbols of rhythm and percussion in the music world.

CHAPTER 46

Pandit Bhimsen Joshi and Dr Balamurali Krishna

What else can you expect but sheer magic when the two greatest singers of both the systems of Indian classical music come together? This recording is undoubtedly a collector's item. The understanding and coordination between the two singers are truly uncanny. The technique, musical skill and presentation in vocal duets by these two giants is unparalleled. Although many attempts were made after this collaboration by many other vocalists, this combination was a league apart with some unconventional and new explorations. This is a live recording from a concert that took place at Shivaji Park, Mumbai, in December 1991 to raise funds for Hari Prasad Chaurasia's music school Gurukul.

THE RECORDING

ALBUM: Jugalbandi (Duet) Series Pandit Bhimsen Joshi and Dr Balamurali Krishna
RAGAS: Darbari Kanhara, Malkauns and Bhairavi
ACCOMPANISTS: Shashikant Muley (tabla), Tulsidas Borkar (harmonium), unknown (violin)
RELEASED BY: Navras Records (1993)

1. Raga Darbari Kanhara: Alaap and composition in teentaal/aditaal
Tansen's magnificent fifteenth century-creation is sung, perhaps even recorded for the first time as a collaborative presentation, by two artistes from Hindustani and Carnatic music systems. Some wonderful voice modulation and techniques are heard by both vocalists. Embellishments and signature Bhimsen Joshi and Balamurali Krishna gamaks are heard from the alaap itself. The composition is set to teentaal (16 beats in the north) and aditaal (8 beats in the south). The lyrics are 'Naath Hari'.

2. Raga Malkauns: Alaap and tarana
Malkauns is called Hindolam in the south Indian system of classical music. The raga is established with supreme genius through various techniques. They sing a tarana (called tillana in the south) after a brief alaap. Some heavyweight improvisation is heard along the way, with some unique displays of voice production. The main foundation of energy for voice production is the good flow of air provided by breathing. In the cases of these greats, the accomplishment of singing is through the musical state of emotions, through their inspiration and thoughts. The tabla and mridangam provide a great base to both the stalwarts.

3. Raga Bhairavi (Bhajan): 'Bhajare Guru Deva'
The concluding Raga Bhairavi is presented at its creative best

in the form of a bhajan. The use of all 12 notes of music is made in the most appropriate manner with their signature interpretations. This is indeed an album that captures a historic moment in Indian classical music.

CHAPTER 47

Ustad Bismillah Khan and Ustad Amjad Ali Khan

The two masters were scheduled to play together in the mid seventies but destiny had other plans. The open-air venue in Bihar, where the concert was to take place, was destroyed in a thunderstorm. Almost 30 years later, they played together in New Delhi at Talkatora Stadium in August 2003. The concert was held in memory of the Indian soldiers who lost their lives at war. We happened to be present at the rehearsal that took place in Bismillah Khan sahib's hotel room in old Delhi. The two of us were rather skeptical about the performance and after the rehearsal, we asked our father how it would work, considering Bismillah Khan's age and the difference in scale between the sarod and the shehnai. To this question, our father gave his usual reply: 'Allah malik hai', God will guide us.

The next day, we saw Bismillah Khan sahib, fit and completely in form, waiting in the greenroom, ready to perform. He did come a few scales down and Abba went up to C sharp, which is very high for the sarod. The concert was a historic collaboration and the stadium was packed with over seven thousand people. It was the first time the sarod and shehnai had come together.

After this, a second duet was scheduled in Kolkata in December 2003 at Science City, which did not go quite as planned. As the concert began, Bismillah Khan sahib felt that his mike was at a lower volume and he could not be heard, to which Abba got the audience to confirm that the shehnai could be heard very well. This misunderstanding continued in Khan sahib's mind and reached a point where he finally put down his shehnai and covered his ears. Poor Abba carried on playing on his own and then wound up with 'Raghupati Raghava Raja Ram', after which the curtains came down.

Since it was Kolkata, the audience started yelling that they wanted a second half as only 45 minutes had passed — around 3,000 people were present and had bought tickets. The organizers persuaded Abba to go back on stage and play the second half by himself. He apologized to the sound engineer, Bishwajit Prasad. What became symbolic was Abba playing Tagore's 'Ekla Cholo Re' at the end of his recital. Till date, we have no idea why Bismillah Khan sahib did this, as we were present in the hall and he was sounding his usual best. There was a lot of press that covered this incident and our father said quite a few things in anger soon after the concert. However, on January 1, 2004, Abba issued a press release saying that whatever had happened was a bad dream and he would like to play once again with Ustad Bismillah Khan. Sadly, he never got the chance. There will never be another Bismillah Khan. The shehnai came and went with him.

THE RECORDING

ALBUM: Ru Ba Ru, 2 CD set
RAGAS: Maru Behag, Chaiti and Dhun, Vaishnav Janato, Ram Dhun, Bhairavi
ACCOMPANISTS: Vijay Ghatey and Nazim Hussain (tabla)
RELEASED BY: Music Today (2005)

DISC ONE

1. Maru Behag

The recording opens with a brief alaap establishing the essence of Maru Behag. The usage of both the madhyams (4th note) is presented with utmost beauty by both artistes. Bismillah Khan sahib starts a very popular composition in teentaal. Some wondrous improvisations and unique confluences take place, which are all unrehearsed. Both maestros present the uniqueness of their respective instruments in the most interesting way, and the tabla players, Vijay Ghatey and Nazim Hussain, present some thrilling solos in interludes.

2. Chaiti and Dhun

The typical regional tunes from Varanasi are heard in this track. The chaiti and dhun show the creative liberties taken by both these stalwarts. It is in tracks like this that you need to read, or rather listen, between the lines of grammar and aesthetics. One hears flashes of ragas like Ghara and Kalawati. The dhun which follows the chaiti is close to Raga Manjh Khamaj. This track is a must-hear.

DISC TWO

1. Vaishnav Janato and Ram Dhun

Two of Mahatma Gandhi's favourite songs are played by the artistes — 'Vaishnav Janato' based in Raga Khamaj and 'Ram Dhun' based in Raga Ghara. 'Vaishnav Janato' is played in the alaap and then the artistes go into further improvisation of the raga. The tablas start with the 'Ram Dhun'. Great interchanges, improvisations and complementing repartees are heard. The tablas give wonderful support to both the artistes.

2. Raga Bhairavi

The undisputed and unmatched finale raga for most Indian classical concerts was chosen here too, to bring the curtain down. Typical vocal music phrases are played by both Amjad Ali Khan and Bismillah Khan. Old compositions of instrumental music are played, followed by a tabla duet that brings the house down.

CHAPTER 48

Ustad Ali Akbar Khan and Pandit Ravi Shankar

These are the two people who reinvented the concept of jugalbandi, or duets. Earlier on, when a father-son or teacher-disciple played together, the protocol was very different, with the junior performer following the senior's lead and waiting for the signal to play. There were times when the student or son just sat through the entire performance without playing at all. The parents and gurus these days are far more lenient, to the extent of giving an equal footing to their progeny or students at concerts.

This was the revolutionary pair that distributed their playing equally and made it interesting for listeners. The impact was thunderous and they were like a house on fire together. They were also brothers-in-law at one point of time and have shared some very magical moments together on stage. The legendary partnership inspired many more sarod-sitar duets back then, and continues to do so even today, especially in Bengal.

THE RECORDING

ALBUM: Jugalbandi Ustad Ali Akbar Khan and Pandit Ravi Shankar
RAGAS: Khamaj and Durga
ACCOMPANISTS: Ustad Alla Rakha (tabla), Nodu Mullick, Narayan Sardesai and Terrence Pease (tanpura)
RECORDED BY: Alam Madina Music Productions at the Palace of Fine Arts, San Francisco
RELEASED BY: Saregama (1983)

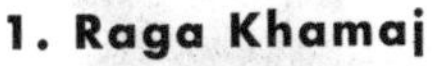

1. Raga Khamaj

The track starts with a fabulous alaap by both the artistes. The understanding and coordination between the sarod and sitar are exceptional. The composition starts in an uplifted tempo of vilambit teentaal. There are some wonderful tabla interludes by the great Ustad Alla Rakha. The lyricism of Khamaj is maintained beautifully, along with some awesome layakari. The drut follows in a very traditional composition that is performed by many instrumentalists. Some interesting tantrakaari is done by both the artistes in this composition. After some fiery improvisations, they come back to the main composition. There is a thrilling climax to this track by all three maestros.

2. Raga Durga

Right from the alaap, the ravishing pentatonic Raga Durga is established in the most appropriate manner. Again, the understanding and coordination between the two artistes is absolutely stunning. The composition is set to jhaptaal and some magical improvisations, along with some creative jugalbandi, are played fabulously. Alla Rakha is at his virtuosic best with some great solo moments.

CHAPTER 49

Ustad Rais Khan and Ustad Sultan Khan

The two maestros have been trendsetters in their respective fields (sitar and sarangi) and have individually carved a niche for themselves. Both have also been associated with the music scene of the Indian film industry from their days in Mumbai, a factor which has influenced them creatively and even personally. Rais Khan sahib and Sultan Khan sahib lived in the same building in Mumbai for years, but never played together until their performance, recorded live, at the Queen Elizabeth Hall, London, in 1993.

Sultan Khan sahib has been a very special person for our family. In 1999, Bharat Bala Productions had taken a group of fifteen musicians to Ladakh for a music video based on the national anthem. Due to fog, the only daily flight to Ladakh at that time could not land for over four days. This was around the time of the Kargil War. We were part of the troupe and spent our time only with Sultan Khan sahib, talking to him from morning till night. When we finally reached the airport on the sixth day, it was as crowded as a fish market, with hundreds of passengers waiting to catch the flight out. A gentleman from the production house informed us that only two tickets were available that day. While we were at the airport, Ayaan had begun feeling a bit uneasy and feverish. Without batting an eyelid, Sultan Khan sahib and Shiv uncle (Shiv Kumar Sharma) gave us their tickets, and we were the only two musicians who travelled out of Ladakh on that flight. Khan sahib even put his tabeez on Ayaan's neck and told him that he would be fine. One never forgets moments like this throughout one's life.

In 2002, Sultan Khan received the Haafiz Ali Khan Award in Gwalior for his contribution to the sarangi. The award was presented by the then Vice-president, Krishna Kant. We also spent time with Sultan Khan sahib in Stuttgart during a nightlong concert in 2001. Whenever Khan sahib has met us, he has been full of warmth. With his great wit and humour, he is the darling of every festival and label.

THE RECORDING

ALBUM: Raag Rang (Recorded live at the Queen Elizabeth Hall, London)
RAGAS: Ragamala and Bhairavi
ARTISTES: Ustad Rais Khan (sitar)
Ustad Sultan Khan (sarangi)
ACCOMPANISTS: Anindo Chatterjee (tabla), Krishna Joshi and Uma Mehta (tanpura)
RELEASED BY: Navras Records (2005)

This is a very special recording and marks the first time that the sitar and sarangi come together. It shows both artistes at their creative best. The ragamala is based on Raga Khamaj. Although there are no rules as such in presenting a ragamala, the tendency is usually to stick to ragas within the same notes. But here the two artistes have created a painting with colours coming in from all sides of the spectrum. From Khamaj, they move to Mian ki Malhar, Jaijaiwanti, Kafi, Darbari, Basant Bahar, Shahana, Kedara, Charukeshi, Shankara, Behag, Sohini, Malkauns and a few more variations. Some great moments are created on stage with the collective musical approaches of both the greats. Anindo Chatterjee provides phenomenal support throughout this piece and also plays some exciting solos.

The recording ends with Raga Bhairavi. This raga is the ideal finale for Indian classical concerts and though it is a morning raga, it is often used as the concluding piece at night concerts. The raga allows the use of all twelve notes, though they must be used in an appealing manner. This piece is packed with lyrical expressions from the sitar and the sarangi, with some interesting dialogues between both artistes. The composition is in teentaal.

CHAPTER 50

Ustad Vilayat Khan and Ustad Bismillah Khan

This was another pair that worked like a house on fire. The first time a duet was announced between the sitar and the shehnai, people were sceptical about how it would work, since the two instruments come from divergent backgrounds and have completely different sounds and styles. However, when the duet did take place, it was a new chapter in the partnership between Vilayat Khan and Bismillah Khan. The two ustads had the highest regard for each other. In fact, Bismillah Khan often said on stage that while he surpassed Vilayat Khan in age, it was Vilayat Khan who was the greater artiste.

The two have quite a few recordings together, but we present here

a live concert that took place in Mumbai at Nehru Centre in the late eighties. We attended only one of their duets in 1993 in New Delhi's Siri Fort auditoruim for the Rajiv Gandhi Foundation. They had played Raga Purba (Puriya Kalyan to the traditional ear) followed by Anandi and Bhairavi.

THE RECORDING

NAME: Great Jugalbandis: Ustad Vilayat Khan and Ustad Bismillah Khan
RAGA: Yaman, Nand Kalyan and Mishra Dhun
ACCOMPANISTS: Nazim Hussain (tabla) and Ustad Bismillah Khan's party
RELEASED BY: Saregama (1989)

1. Raga Yaman

Alaap and composition in teentaal

The evergreen Raga Yaman, when played by masters like these, takes a celestial form. The artistes take the musical liberty of using the shuddha madhyam frugally, hence making it Yaman Kalyan. This thrilling composition is set to sixteen beats. Some spell-binding interactions take place between the two artistes, creating magical moments. Both are at their musical and technical best. As the composition builds tempo, it is very interesting to hear the way both the artistes approach the crescendo, keeping the character of their instruments in mind, without diluting the music.

2. Raga Nand Kalyan

Alaap and gat in teentaal

The traditional Anandi Kalyan is called Nand Kalyan here. Typical vocal phrases are played by both the musical giants. It's like poetry being created on the spot. The composition is a very popular one of Anandi Kalyan. The phrase Ga Ma Dha Pa Re Sa Ga is the epicentre of the piece, set to sixteen beats. The improvisations are done in turns. There is a heavy element of exchanges and musical counterparts. One can hear and sense the artistes' mutual admiration for each other as they play.

3. Mishra Dhun in Kehrwa

A typically traditional tune is played in a lighter form of classical music. A lot of rhythmic interplays are heard, with the imagination of both the masters reigning supreme. Typical vocal phrases are played both on the shehnai and the sitar. Again, the thin line between grammar and poetry is revealed.

Afterword

I am honoured to be invited to provide this afterword by two musicians and rising stars I have known and admired for some fourteen years. Their father and guru, Ustaad Amjad Ali Khan, and his own father and guru, Ustad Haafiz Ali Khan, figure prominently among the fifty greatest, as is to be expected. As torchbearers of the family tradition stretching back over seven generations, we have every reason to hope that in the not too distant future, Amaan and Ayaan will be listed among the outstanding senior practitioners of the art. The pages of this book give some idea of how much they are steeped in music and how much they have imbibed, often at first hand, from the great musicians they have selected.

My task is rather like that of a humble composer attempting a coda to a set of fifty grand variations on the noblest of themes, keeping to the style of what has come before. How can all the variations be tied up in a synthesis or apotheosis? How can the great theme be brought back to crown the whole work? I should not even try such an ambitious encroachment on the art of these legendary musicians. The central theme is Indian classical music and no epilogue is needed to demonstrate the enduring greatness of that tradition. Most of the names brought to our attention so sympathetically and respectfully are very well known throughout the world. Each has made a significant contribution and helped define twentieth-century Indian classical music — a period of great change, affecting the ideas, content and presentation of the music to mass audiences, both in India and around the world. How difficult it must have been to limit the number to fifty, especially when both strands of Indian classical music — the northern (Hindustani) and the southern (Carnatic) — must be surveyed. By confining the study to the twentieth century and the age of recording, the task has been made somewhat more manageable. For me, trying to select not only the fifty greatest Western singers and instrumentalists but also the composers of the same century (bearing in mind that an Indian musician is usually all three in one) would be a daunting task, inevitably giving rise to a debate about who has been included and who omitted. With Indian music the task is surely no less demanding and the debate no less heated.

One criterion in this book has centred on recording. The many legends before the twentieth century are not here and there is no way of hearing them. Some of the names included flourished in the earliest phase of the recording era and there are not many good recordings readily available, but still we can hear something to get an idea of their stature, bearing in mind that those in their final years may have no longer been at quite the height of their powers. Another criterion is personal acquaintance, though not applied across the board, as it would have limited the options too much. Biographies of the great artists are easy to come by, but not so the personal reminiscences of these two authors, stretching back into early childhood. Such accounts are not only unique but also of enormous value. Notice how the earliest musical memories of Amaan and Ayaan were of their father (one of the leading instrumentalists of our time) singing to them. Indian music is really founded on singing, with all the expressiveness and flexibility that the voice conveys, and instrumentalists sing through their instruments and, just as importantly, away from them as well. It comes as no surprise, therefore, to see that almost half of the artistes selected were or are singers. Their names may not be as familiar around the world as some of the famous instrumentalists featured, but in India they remain beacons of music's essence. Becoming acquainted with their singing promises to be a special revelation and pleasure for listeners who are relatively new to Indian music.

So, my task of drawing all the strands together in one grand finale has proved impossible. Instead, I resort to a wondrous contemplation of the vast meadow from which these flowers have been collected, surrounded by countless others. When beauty is all around, it is easy to take it for granted. May that never happen. May one golden age be validated by untiring efforts to create others, both through respectful adherence to the unique tradition and ceaseless creativity and innovation.

NEIL SORRELL
UNIVERSITY OF YORK

Acknowledgements

This book has been conceived, planned and evolved by our dear friend Neelini Sarkar of HarperCollins, who is a fine sitar player herself. She has a tremendous feeling for music and has been truly passionate about the book till the very end. Thank you, Lali!

We would also like to thank V.K. Karthika, Publisher and Chief Editor of HarperCollins for taking so much interest in this book. We would like to thank all the recording labels for their support and kind gestures, especially Saregama for providing the CD that accompanies the book.

A big thank you must go to Shubhani Sarkar for her beautiful and inspired artwork.

We must express our special gratitude to Dr Deepthi Omcherry Bhalla for her invaluable inputs. She has played a vital role in many aspects of this work and we thank her from the core of our hearts.

We would like to thank Professor Neil Sorrell from the University of York for writing the most beautiful afterword. We would also like to thank Dr Deepak Chopra for writing us such a wonderful endorsement.

A big thank you must go to Mr Mukul Kansal and Ms Shikha Rawal for all the support and assistance with the precious recordings at Saregama.

Thank you Mr Vibhaker Baxi at Navras Records for all the cooperation and help. Thank you Chhanda Dhara, Universal Music, Music Today, Mr S.L. Saha of Hindusthan Music, Mr Igor Wakhevitch for Radio France, Mr Rangasami Parthasarthy of Oriental Records, Asit Ghatak, Radha Viswanathan, daughter and disciple of M.S. Subbulakshmi, Sudha Ranganathan, Phil Dent, Rakesh Prasanna, Suji Yamamoto, Tanmoy Bose, Mithlesh Kumar Jha, Revathy Venkataraman, Janaki Nathan, Pushpa Shankar, David Murphy, Rupam Ghosh, Kavita

Chibber and Nuri Naqvi, Director General, All India Radio.

Thank you Ananda Bazar Patrika for the precious photographs and the Haafiz Ali Khan Memorial Trust for the photographs from the Haafiz Ali Khan Music Festivals (1973–1979).

Lastly, thank you Ma and Abba for your continued faith in us during the hard times in our lives. And Neema, thank you for the patience, support and coffee.